Cheese

HOW TO CHOOSE, SERVE & ENJOY

Cheese Fondue (page 71)

By the Editors of Sunset Books
and Sunset Magazine

Lane Publishing Co. • Menlo Park, California

RESEARCH & TEXT
BOB THOMPSON

DEVELOPMENTAL EDITOR
HELEN SWEETLAND

COORDINATING EDITOR
CORNELIA FOGLE

DESIGN
WILLIAMS & ZILLER DESIGN

PHOTOGRAPHERS

Victor Budnik: 4, 7, 8, 9, 10, 12, 13, 14, 15, 16, 17, 18, 19, 20, 21, 22, 23, 24, 25, 26, 27, 28, 29, 30, 31, 59, 62, 83, 91. **Kathryn Kleinman:** 51. **Michael Lamotte:** 2. **Darrow M. Watt:** 1, 86. **Tom Wyatt:** 70, 75, 78. **Nikolay Zurek:** 32, 35, 38, 43, 46, 54, 67, 94.

PHOTO STYLISTS

Karen Hazarian: 10, 12, 13, 14, 15, 16, 17, 18, 19, 20, 21, 22, 23, 24, 25, 26, 27, 28, 29, 30, 31, 62, 91. **JoAnn Masaoka:** 4, 7, 8, 9, 46, 59, 70, 83. **James McNair:** 2. **Lynne B. Morrall:** 1, 32, 35, 38, 43, 51, 54, 67, 75, 78, 94. **Elizabeth Ross:** 86.

SAY CHEESE!

Slice it, dice it, melt it, spread it; serve it hot or cold, alone or combined with myriad other foods—it's hard to imagine anything that can match the variety, versatility, and nutritional goodness of cheese.

Explore the fascinating world of cheese with us, as we take you step-by-step through the cheesemaking process. Then, discover over 175 varieties of cheese, both domestic and imported, in our detailed reference guide. Finally, turn to our recipe chapter, where you'll find plenty of choices for every course and every occasion—whether you're preparing a simple appetizer, a hearty main dish, or a luscious, rich dessert.

For sharing their knowledge of cheeses and cheesemaking, we thank Dick Allen of The Wine & Cheese Center, San Francisco; Mary Ellen Allen of The Village Cheese Shop, Houston; the entire cheese department of Balducci's, New York City; Jim Brooks and Pierce Thompson of Marin French Cheese Factory, Petaluma, California; Laura Chenel of Laura Chenel's California Chèvre, Santa Rosa, California; Allen Gordon of Marshall Fields, Chicago; the Italian Trade Commission, New York City; Paula Lambert of The Mozzarella Company, Dallas; Barbara Lang of Inglenook Vineyards, Rutherford, California; Mary Lyons of Food & Wines from France, New York City; Jo Ann Parsons of Safeway Stores, Dallas; Phillip S. Quattrociocchi of San Francisco International Cheese Imports, San Francisco; Daryl Sattui of V. Sattui, St. Helena, California; and Ignazio A. Vella of Vella Cheese Company, Sonoma, California.

Special thanks to Jim Brooks, Pierce Thompson, and Ignazio Vella for opening their cheese factories to our photographers. For providing some of the cheeses shown in the "Gallery of Famous Cheeses," we are grateful to Laura Chenel's California Chèvre, Domestic Cheese Company, Kendall Cheese Company, and San Francisco International Cheese Imports. And for their generosity in sharing some of the props used in our photographs, we extend our thanks to The Best of All Worlds, Menlo Park Hardware, and Williams-Sonoma.

Finally, not the least of our thanks to Elizabeth Friedman for selecting the recipes and preparing the food for some of the photographs.

Cover: Design by Williams & Ziller. Photograph by Victor Budnik. Photo styling by Karen Hazarian.

Sunset Books
    Editor: David E. Clark
    Managing Editor: Elizabeth L. Hogan

First printing September 1986

Spread ripe pears with creamy Gorgonzola or other blue cheese (see pages 12 and 13) for a simple, delicious dessert with coffee.

CONTENTS

HOW CHEESE IS MADE

A cheese begins to acquire its individual character while it is still milk. Beginning at that point, every choice, every step taken, drives each cheese further along its particular path.

The milk. Most cheeses are made from cow's milk; others start with goat's milk (chèvre), sheep's milk (Roquefort, Pecorino Romano), and water buffalo milk (some types of mozzarella). The milk used to make cheese is often pasteurized. U.S. law requires that cheeses made from unpasteurized milk be aged for a minimum of 60 days.

The butterfat content of cheese varies widely. Low-fat cheeses, made from skimmed or partially skimmed milk, may have butterfat contents as low as 5 percent. Whole-milk cheeses have 45 to 55 percent butterfat. Double-cream cheeses must have enough cream added to give 60 percent butterfat; triple creams must have a minimum of 75 percent butterfat. (Exactly how the percent of butterfat corresponds to amount of fat is a vexing question for weight watchers, since fat content is measured as a percentage of milk solids, not of the whole cheese. See page 17.)

Before it is made into cheese, milk is usually conditioned with a starter—a culture of microbes that causes the curds to ferment. The exact nature of this starter gives each cheese its particular flavor and texture. Some starters also increase the acidity of the milk.

Separating curds. The actual making of cheese begins with renneting, the addition of an enzyme that acts on milk to separate solid curds from liquid whey. All but a few cheeses begin with it.

To make some cheeses, the milk is "cooked"—heated to about 100° F—while the curds are forming. Because heating causes some moisture to evaporate, cooked cheeses are usually firm or hard in texture, Cheddar and Swiss being classic examples. However, some of the softer cheeses such as mozzarella and jack are cooked, too.

Once the curds have formed, the cheese is ready to be shaped and cured—except in the case of *fresh cheeses*, which are simply scooped into containers and marketed. Cottage cheese is the prime example of a fresh cheese.

(Continued on next page)

Ignazio Vella, a master cheesemaker at 28 and now the head of his family's firm, shows off a wheel of dry jack. Vella's is one of only two companies making this delicious but often overlooked eating or grating cheese.

Shaping and curing. All cheeses not meant to be eaten fresh must be cured. Before they reach that step, however, they are given their shape and basic texture.

Unpressed cheeses are formed, then left to drain naturally. Most soft cheeses are unpressed.

Pressed cheeses don't lose moisture simply by draining—liquid is squeezed out of the curds after they're placed in their forms. Many firm and almost all hard cheeses are pressed.

Spun curd, or *pasta filata* in Italian, defines a cheese textured and shaped by kneading and stretching the curd in warmed whey or water. Mozzarella and string cheese are typical examples.

At the curing stage, the flavoring starter culture is allowed to come to full flower, giving each cheese its identity. As a general rule, firm and hard cheeses ripen slowly, acquiring familiar, easily likeable flavors, while soft and semisoft ones ripen quickly, developing stronger flavors and aromas.

The chart below groups most of the familiar cheeses by degree of firmness and intensity of flavor. On the following pages we show the basic steps in making jack, Cheddar, and soft cheeses.

THE TEXTURES & FLAVORS OF CHEESE

This chart groups some of the cheeses discussed in this book on the basis of texture and intensity of flavor. However, there are many things the chart *can't* do. For example, though it shows that both Stilton and Limburger have plenty of flavor, it can't explain that they don't taste at all like each other. Nor can it explain that, though Pont l'Évêque and Port du Salut appear in the same little box, the former is almost always stronger than the latter. (Our 4 flavor categories are a graphic convenience; the flavor scale is obviously a continuum.) For fuller descriptions of the cheeses above and many others, see pages 12 to 31.

TYPE OF TEXTURE		INTENSITY OF FLAVOR OR AROMA			
		Very mild	**Mild**	**Strong**	**Very strong**
SOFT	Loose curds	Cottage cheese Mascarpone Ricotta			
	Runs or oozes		Brie (fresh)	Brie (ripe) Camembert	
	Readily spreadable	Cream cheese Farmers cheese	Boursault Boursin	Blue Castello Oregon Blue Pipo Crem'	Gorgonzola Stilton
	Crumbles as spread			Danish Blue Roquefort	
SEMISOFT	Clings to knife	Münster (American)	Bel Paese	Chèvre Crescenza Pont l'Évêque Port du Salut Taleggio	Beer Cheese Esrom Limburger Münster (Alsatian) Oka
	Springy; can be sliced	American string cheese Jack Mozzarella	Caciocavallo Havarti Provolone		
FIRM	Slices smoothly	Cheshire Colby	Appenzeller Cheddar (mild) Edam & Gouda Gruyère Leyden Raclette	Emmenthaler Fontal Fontina d'Aosta	
	Crumbles as sliced		Cougar Gold	Cheddar (sharp) Feta	
HARD	Hard enough to grate	American Parmesan	Asiago Dry jack Kasseri Sbrinz	Parmigiano Reggiano Pecorino	

MAKING JACK CHEESE

Jack comes in two forms, regular and dry. Much of the difference is in the makeup of the starter. Otherwise, all the steps except aging are very much the same.

The cheesemaker adds a starter culture to the milk, and adds rennet shortly thereafter. The milk soon curdles, forming a soft blanket atop the whey. This blanket is cut into cubes, which sink into slightly warmed whey. When the whey is drained off, the cubes have a slightly stiffer consistency than cottage cheese.

After the curds have been gathered along one side of the tank, the cheesemaker measures them into cloth squares using a stainless steel bucket (photo 1). Workers roll the bag of new cheese against the tank to pack the curd as closely as they can (photo 2); then they tie the bag closed. Next, the new cheese goes through a press to pack it tighter and squeeze out more whey (photo 3). Then it is unwrapped and stored flat until it becomes firm enough to handle.

Once firm, each cheese goes into a brief brine bath (photo 4). After the bath, the cheese is stored on edge for a few days or weeks of curing. (Storing young cheeses on edge ensures even ripening.)

Dry jack goes through an extra step. After initial curing, it is coated with a mixture of oil, cocoa, and pepper (photo 5), then put back on racks for the slow aging that makes it hard enough to grate (photo 6).

1

2

3

4

5

6

MAKING CHEDDAR

A cooked, pressed cheese, Cheddar is distinct from all others in being made with a starter organism that causes the curds to mat densely as they form. Some Cheddars get their characteristic golden color from a flavorless dye made from annatto seeds, which is added at the same time as the starter (photo 1). White Cheddars go without this step.

Shortly after the starter is added, the milk is renneted. The milk forms a solid blanket atop the whey, just as it does when jack cheese is made. The blanket is cubed with a wire knife (photo 2). The Cheddar curds sink into whey warmed from about 104°F (for mild cheese) to about 112°F (for sharp cheese). They "cook" for 2¼ hours, during which time they become curiously rubbery in texture and firmer than the curds for most other cheeses.

At the proper time, the whey is drawn off, leaving the curds to mat in the bottom of the tank (photo 3).

When they reach the proper texture, the curds are cut into loaves and turned to help drain away whey (photo 4). This cutting and turning is repeated several times. After the last cutting and turning, the loaves are cut into strips by rotary knives (photo 5). Next, the cut curds are packed into telescoping hoops (photo 6), weighed, and pressed.

Removed from the hoops, the new Cheddars age for several months (for mild cheese) to more than a year (for sharp cheese).

1

2

3

MAKING SOFT CHEESES

Soft cheeses are generally uncooked and unpressed. Their starters develop flavors swiftly, so the aging process usually takes well under a month. A single starter with more than one active organism can be used to make two quite different cheeses from the same batch of renneted milk.

As the curd forms in milk held at about 95°F, it is gently stirred to keep it in small chunks about the consistency of soft yogurt *(photo 1)*. When it has reached the proper consistency, it is poured into molds, where it is allowed to drain *(photo 2)*.

After it has been turned several times and drained to firmness, the new cheese goes into a brine bath—a short bath for mild flavors, a longer one for more intense flavors *(photo 3)*.

At this point, the cheesemaker determines the final character of the cheese by controlling the environment in which it cures. To make a Brie-type, the cheese goes into warm, relatively dry surroundings, where a yeast forms the familiar powdery white bloom on the unworked surface *(photo a4)*.

To make a washed-rind type, such as Schloss, the cheese is sprayed with water at regular intervals *(photo b4)* and the moist surface is rubbed to help a flavoring bacteria work its way into the surface *(photo b5)*. A moist surface encourages bacterial growth and inhibits yeast; a dry surface works in the opposite way.

a4

b4

b5

A GALLERY OF ◄ FAMOUS ► CHEESES

In this chapter, we've gathered most of the well-known cheeses of the world into just 14 families—both for easy reference and for easy comparison.

Families can be funny—the gangly redhead will show up amid a host of compact brunets. However, most of the cheeses in any one family in this section have similar enough flavors and textures to make them recognizable as a group. Substitutions are easy, then, for someone who wants a change of cheese, but only a small change.

Of all the families, the Swiss and Swiss-types are most alike. All are firm, and all share flavors that are at once faintly nutty and faintly piquant. The Cheddars and their cousins are almost as reliable in character, though some English cheeses are made from riper (or sharper) milk, and so are nippier than a mild Cheddar. The blues, while they vary in some important details, are all dominated by the flavorful mold *Penicillium roqueforti*. And so it goes . . . with one major exception.

That exception is the group of cheeses labeled here as "Monastery Cheeses & Beyond." All of these are semisoft; all ripen from the outside inwards, so their aromas are concen-

trated more at the rind than in the paste. But talk about the Hatfields and the McCoys! Port du Salut does not smell at all like Münster, nor Münster anything like Beer Cheese. In short, some are powerful, others mild. In the cases of most families, it is a matter of like one, like them all; but with the semisofts, this does not hold true.

Family resemblances aside, the selection of cheeses within each group attempts to give some subtle choices of flavor. When you begin to try these cheeses, you may notice some differences in price, as well. The most famous members of each tribe usually cost dearly, while some of their lesser-known kin are just as pleasing and sell for much less.

The selection also tries to keep at least some focus on cheeses made by specialists and craftsmen in the United States and Canada. A small renaissance in farmhouse cheesemaking has caught hold in North America. While the results have been excellent in all parts of the continent, the choices here represent largely Western cheesemakers. (The limited production of the small number of such craftsmen often means that sales are limited to local or, at best, regional markets.)

A deli case full of cheeses
of every size, shape, and color
may seem a bit daunting.
However, the flavors and textures
of most of the world's cheeses divide neatly
into only a dozen or so families.

BLUE CHEESES

Though all blue cheeses share the basic flavor of *Penicillium roqueforti*, different milks make them individually distinctive. Collectively among the greatest eating cheeses, blues offer variety in both texture (ranging from readily spreadable to crumbly) and flavor (ranging from delicate and only slightly tangy to richly earthy and very sharp indeed). The milder ones are most familiar as a flavoring ingredient in salad dressings. However, all of them melt well in pasta dishes, omelets, crêpes, and soufflés, though it's important to remember that most liquefy quickly and completely when subjected to high heat.

Buying and storing: The moister the cheese, the faster it ripens (or overripens). Darkened, gray-brown areas in the paste indicate that a blue is past its prime. Other signs of over-age include discolored wrapping from oozing moisture and an overstrong to ammoniated smell. Refrigerate in lightly waxed paper or plastic wrap.

GORGONZOLA

Northern Italy's great blue-veined cheese comes in two forms—the long-aged, powerfully aromatic traditional one, and the milder, though hardly bland, *Dolcelatte (sweet Gorgonzola)*. In both, pronounced mold flavors play against ripely cheesy ones. Gorgonzola is moist enough to spread before it crumbles.

ROQUEFORT

To bear the name, Roquefort must be made of sheep's milk from a defined area and must be aged in particular caves in the south of France. In this distinctive cheese, unusually subtle hints of blue mold mingle with the piquant flavor of sheep's milk. More often than not, Roquefort tastes the saltiest of the blues. Though so soft that it melts on the tongue, Roquefort is dry enough to crumble more readily than it spreads.

STILTON

One of the great British cheeses, Stilton is distinct from all other blues for being based in a cheddared cheese, and it keeps an unmistakable smack of that as a background to its blue mold flavors. Like Cheddar, it grows sharper and stronger with age. Unlike Cheddar, it shares with Gorgonzola a creamy, spreadable softness.

AMERICAN BLUES

Among the dozen or so blues made in the U.S., two of the most distinctive are identified by place names. *Maytag Blue* (bottom right), from a single farm in Iowa, has a creamy texture, pronounced blue flavors, and a definite piquancy. *Oregon Blue* (top) is also rich in blue flavors but not quite as tangy as the Maytag Blue. *Treasure Cave*, from Minnesota, is milder than either. California's *Kendall Chèvreblue* (bottom left) is a goat's milk blue and, predictably, tangiest of them all. *Blue Moon New World*, from Wisconsin, tastes plenty blue but doesn't look it, since it's flavored by a variant strain of white mold.

MORE FRENCH BLUES

In addition to Roquefort, the French make several fine cow's milk blues. The crumbly *Bleu d'Auvergne* (right) is one of the bluest in color of all blues. Also from the Auvergne region of France is a similar cheese called *Bleu de Salers*, made from the milk of the Salers breed of cow. *Bleu de Bresse* (lower left), named after a town not far north of Lyon, is piquant, creamy textured, and less heavily veined than the Auvergne blues.

SCANDINAVIAN BLUES

Danish Blue (right) is another pungent cheese that's flavored and textured perfectly for crumbling over salads or into dressings. *Mycella*, also Danish, is milder. *Blue Castello* (left), yet another Danish product, is a double cream (almost a triple, actually, at 72 percent butterfat) to be sought as much for its soft, spreadable richness as its blue flavor.

BLUE HYBRIDS

Bavarian Blue (left) and Denmark's *Saga* intentionally marry techniques used in making two distinctive types of cheeses—the bloomy rinds (see pages 14 and 15) and the blues. The French *Pipo Crem'* (right) is said to grow its bloomy rind spontaneously. All double creams with 65 to 72 percent butterfat, these cheeses begin creamy-soft and age ever softer in the way of Camembert.

BRIE, CAMEMBERT & COMPANY

Among the soft-ripened cheeses, Brie and Camembert are the most famous. Also called "bloomy rinds," these cheeses are flavored by a mold that leaves a powdery white bloom on their surfaces as they age. Bloomy rinds have the curious quality of ripening rapidly as long as the wheel is not cut—and ripening little or not at all after it is. These cheeses are perfect for spreading on crackers or sliced fruit, for deep-frying in chunks, or for using as fillings in omelets and crêpes. Any bloomy rind also makes an excellent choice for a cheese board that's served as the last course of a fine meal, in the European tradition.

Buying and storing: Best bought cut from ripe, whole wheels, bloomy rinds spoil quickly and so are meant for immediate use. Perfectly ripened (in as little time as a month after manufacture), these cheeses just begin to ooze. Overripe (as early as 3 months), they are runny and smell of ammonia. Underripe bloomy rinds have a stiff, chalky center. Refrigerate in lightly waxed paper or plastic wrap. Bring to room temperature before serving.

BRIE

The original Brie, thin and pie-sized, comes from an area near the village of Brie, south and east of Paris. What the French think of as great Brie cannot be exported legally to the United States, because it is made from unpasteurized milk and cured less than the 60 days U.S. law requires. True examples of these cheeses—*Brie de Meaux* and *Brie de Melun*—have richer flavors than their more polite, exportable cousins made from pasteurized milk. The latter are called just *Brie* (top) or *Brie de Coulommiers*. (Just to confuse the issue, a pasteurized Brie de Meaux can also be found in the U.S.) All Bries start out relatively mild and grow stronger in flavor as they mature.

Recent years have brought a vogue for flavored Brie. Mushrooms, herbs (bottom left), and pepper (bottom right) are some of the more common seasonings. Purists frown, but purists often do.

CAMEMBERT

Camembert is the name of a village in the heart of Normandy, and also of a cheese that tastes much like Brie. Camemberts are more pointed in flavor and richer in texture than traditional Brie, however; in general, they're also smaller in diameter and thicker.

OTHER FRENCH BLOOMY RINDS

The names Brie and Camembert dominate the field of soft-ripened cheeses in France, but a few others are well established. The Brie-like *Coulommiers* (shown in photo) and *Carré de l'Est* are the best known among them. They're often a little less expensive than Brie and Camembert.

AMERICAN BLOOMY RINDS

American-made soft-ripened cheeses generally go by the names Brie and Camembert. A French company makes a Brie type in Wisconsin. A California company makes both Brie (right) and Camembert (left) types. The latter cheeses behave somewhat differently from their French cousins; as they ripen, they maintain a less liquid, less oozing texture. Their flavors are similar to the French originals but fresher and less pungent.

SOFT-RIPENED DOUBLE CREAMS

The general theory of double creams seems to be that you cannot have too much of a good thing. Double-cream bloomy rinds are—predictably—even more unctuous in texture than fully ripe Camemberts. In compensation, they are not quite as aromatic—or as flavorful. French brands dominate, including *Délice de France* (top), *Folie du Chef, Marquis de Cremembert* (bottom), *Revidoux, Rondeau, Rose d'Or*, and *St. Honoré*. Not incidentally, it pays to read the fine print on labels of cheeses called just "Brie" or "Camembert"; some are double creams, with 60 percent butterfat or more.

France does not own the field of soft-ripened double creams. *Vecchia Baita* is a popular example from Italy. Denmark's contribution, *Crema Danica*, is seldom seen on the West Coast, but it's sometimes available in the eastern U.S.

SOFT-RIPENED TRIPLE CREAMS

If double cream is not enough. . . . *L'Explorateur* (right) is the best-known of the bloomy-rind triple creams from France. Its primary competitors are *St. André* (left), *Brillat-Savarin*, and *Gratte Paille*. Still more unctuous than the double creams, they are more memorable for texture than bloomy-rind flavor.

CHEDDARS

Cheddar, like Champagne, names both a place and a process. The name comes from a town in England. The process (see page 8), widespread in English cheesemaking, went abroad with colonists beginning in the 1700s, especially to North America, Australia, and New Zealand. In the United States alone, fine Cheddars are produced in such diverse corners of the country as Vermont, New York, Wisconsin, Oregon, and California. There's little need to tell any U.S. citizen over the age of 10 how to use Cheddar. It is by far the most-bought, most-eaten, most-cooked-with cheese in the nation. The only serious question is how thick to cut it for sandwiches.

Buying and storing: Avoid cheeses with darkened, dried, cracked spots in the paste. Firm Cheddars ripen slowly, so they can be kept for a month or more. Refrigerate in lightly waxed paper or plastic wrap.

MILD CHEDDAR

Mild Cheddars cure for well under a year (usually no more than 4 months), so they're moister than sharp Cheddars as well as being mild-flavored. Mild Cheddars offer an easy-to-like flavor and an eminently sliceable, shreddable, and meltable texture—characteristics that have made them by far the most popular cheeses in the United States. They may be orange-gold from a vegetable dye (right) or their natural pale ivory hue (left). The dye does not change the flavor (see page 8).

SHARP CHEDDAR

From the beginning, sharp Cheddars are drier, sharper, and more pungently flavored than mild ones. As they cure (usually upwards of 6 months, sometimes for a year), they slowly become still sharper, drier, and more crumbly. Like mild Cheddars, the sharp cheeses may be either orange-gold (left) or ivory (right). *English Farmhouse Cheddar* remains the standard by which sharp Cheddars are measured.

CHEDDAR'S AMERICAN RELATIVES

Cheddar has several American relatives. One, *Colby*, looks and tastes like a particularly mild Cheddar. Another, *Cougar Gold* (shown in photo), has a Cheddar-like texture and is made very much as Cheddars are, but with a different starter culture that gives it a sweeter character and a faintly nutty flavor. It is sold in sealed tins and will keep indefinitely until the tin is opened.

CHEDDAR'S ENGLISH COUSINS

The numerous firm cheeses from the United Kingdom have not gained widespread popularity in the United States, even though most are close cousins to Cheddar. *Caerphilly* (top), originally from Wales, is pale, moist, and subtly flavored, but among the most piquant of firm cheeses despite only brief aging. *Wensleydale* is much like it. (Some say these two cheeses taste exactly like buttermilk.) Pale gold, slightly salty *Cheshire* is also quite piquant, but it's closer to a mild Cheddar in flavor. *Gloucester* (bottom) is a closer match to sharp Cheddar than the others. Most of the pale ivory, pale-flavored cheese called *Derby* comes into the U.S. as *Sage Derby* (center), with the herb serving as both a coloring and a flavoring agent.

Like cheesemakers in other countries, the British have taken to combining and flavoring traditional cheeses for the novelty of it. Examples include *Huntsman*, which combines layers of Stilton and Gloucester, and *Walton*, which mixes Stilton and Cheddar and is covered with walnuts.

CHEESE, DIET & DIET CHEESE

The plain fact is, cream and salt give cheese its texture and its ability to develop flavor. The less cream and salt used, the less "cheesy" the final product.

Most whole-milk cheeses have 45 to 55 percent butterfat and 1 to 2 percent sodium. At the upper extreme for fat are triple creams, which have a *minimum* of 75 percent butterfat (double creams range from 60 to 74 percent butterfat). For salt, the top figure is about 9 percent.

The salt figure is always a percent of total weight, but the figure for fat is not. Butterfat percentages state the amount of fat as a percent of milk solids in the cheese, *not* as a percent of total weight. For this reason, firm cheeses (up to 70 percent solid/30 percent liquid) have more fat than soft cheeses (30 percent solid/70 percent liquid) of the same butterfat percentage. For example, while a Brie of 50 percent butterfat has a shade less than 8 grams of fat per ounce, a Cheddar of 50 percent butterfat has slightly over 9 grams of fat per ounce.

If you're looking for a cheese with butterfat content even lower than 45 percent, you have the following options (among others).

- **Fresh cheeses:** *Low-fat cottage cheese* (between 1 and 5 percent butterfat); *farmers cheese* (between 5 and 45 percent butterfat)
- **Grating type:** *Sap Sago* (no butterfat)
- **Soft-ripened cheeses:** *St. Felice* (5 percent butterfat); *St. Otho* (9 percent butterfat)
- **Swiss types:** *Low-fat Danbo* (10 percent butterfat); *Lorraine Swiss* (18 percent butterfat); *Montvalay* (20 percent butterfat)

If you're trying to cut down on sodium, you'll want to remember that most kinds of cheese contain a fair amount. There is some variation, though: for example, American cheese contains 406 milligrams of sodium per ounce, while natural Cheddar has 176 and cream cheese just 84. Cheeses labeled "low sodium" are probably your best bet —*low-sodium Gouda*, for example, has just 7 milligrams per ounce.

FETA CHEESES

The original feta was a sheep's milk cheese made in the Balkans, especially Greece. Now produced in many countries, it is often made from a mixture of sheep's and goat's milk, or goat's and cow's milk; sometimes it is made from cow's milk alone.

Buying and storing: Feta should be bought and used as young and moist as possible. To slow its aging, some feta fanciers store it in a brine that can be bought with the cheese.

FETA

Its manner of curing—4 to 6 weeks in a brine bath—distinguishes feta from all other cheeses. From that comes its soft, crumbly texture and its strong, salty flavor. Everybody knows that feta crumbles onto Mediterranean salads. Fewer know that, if properly moist, it may also melt beautifully. Most imported feta comes from Italy, not Greece; well-regarded ones also come from Germany and Bulgaria.

FONTINA & FRIENDS

True fontina, a single cheese made in northern Italy, now heads an international family of cheeses called by several similar names. It makes a fine eating cheese and is versatile in cooking.

Buying and storing: Ripe fontina is full-flavored, firm, almost as crumbly as sharp Cheddar, and pale ivory. When underripe, it is bland, springy, and moist—somewhat like jack. Most fontinas you'll find at the market fall in between. Refrigerate in lightly waxed paper or plastic wrap.

FONTINA D'AOSTA

The original fontina, this cheese is made only from unpasteurized milk, and only in the Aosta Valley of northern Italy. The initials CPF ("Consortium of Fontina Producers") appear on each wheel. Techniques used to make fontina resemble those used for Swiss cheeses; however, a very different starter culture produces distinctive flavors and only a few tiny holes. Depending on age, fontina can be mild and milky, faintly nutty, or memorably complicated in flavor.

FONTAL

Fontal is also Italian, but it is produced in a wider area of the country and is made from pasteurized milk. At its best, it comes very close to Fontina d'Aosta, though it isn't quite as full-flavored. A good eating cheese, it also melts particularly well in baked dishes. Some merchants sell fontal as fontina.

FONTINA TYPES FROM ELSEWHERE

Several European countries have imitated fontina with some success. *Swedish fontina* (left) gets the highest marks from cheese connoisseurs, both for its rich, nutty flavor and its consistently high quality. *Danish fontina* (right) tends to be slightly milder in flavor and moister in texture than its Swedish cousin. A more distant U.S.-made relative, *Fontinella*, may be firmer and drier than well-aged Cheddar, but it stays mild in flavor.

FRESH CHEESES

Fresh cheeses are different from all the others in this gallery in that they are not cured at all. Almost as soon as the curds separate from the whey, out the door these cheeses go. (Even if given the chance, their starters would not produce profoundly cheesy flavors.) Many are good eating cheeses, but they more often serve as ingredients in a wide variety of hot and cold dishes.

Buying and storing: Buy the freshest cheese available. Refrigerate loose-curd cheeses in sealed containers, firmer ones in plastic wrap.

COTTAGE CHEESE

This old American favorite needs no introduction. Everybody knows its milky, mildly piquant flavor and its range of textures from small curd (right) to large (left). Most people eat it straight from the refrigerator—to the dismay of connoisseurs, who know it tastes much richer at room temperature. *Farmers cheese* is essentially cottage cheese pressed into a brick. It has the same flavor but a denser texture.

CREAM CHEESE

One of America's great inventions, cream cheese is a wonderfully rich spread—not to mention an essential ingredient in Old-fashioned Cheesecake (see page 87). Many major brands of cream cheese are stiffened with gum arabic to improve their shelf life, but a few small producers still make a softer, creamier style without the preservative. American *Neufchâtel* is a smoother cream cheese with less butterfat.

FRESH DOUBLE AND TRIPLE CREAMS

The French make several fresh double- and triple-cream cheeses. The most widely imported of these are *Boursin* (left) and *Boursault* (right). Double-cream Boursin is flavored, usually with herbs or coarse-ground pepper; triple-cream Boursault comes plain. Both are so soft they must be packaged in little cups.

(Continued on next page)

MASCARPONE

Mascarpone is best known as the sweet, creamy cheese that's a major ingredient in Italian tortas. It's imported from Italy both as a cheese and as an ingredient in the completed confection.

RICOTTA

Italian ricotta is made from the whey of other cheeses, which gives it the satiny texture so useful in baked pasta dishes and desserts alike. Most American-made ricotta is based on whole or skimmed milk, so it's thicker and curdier than its Italian cousin, making it basically a sweeter cottage cheese. A few small producers in the U.S. follow the original model, however.

PROCESSED CHEESES

All of the cheeses in this gallery are natural cheeses, which is to say they are made directly from milk by separating curds from whey. Processed cheeses, on the other hand, are made primarily from natural cheeses—usually surplus cheeses, or those kept from the market because of defects in appearance.

To make a processed cheese, the natural cheeses are finely ground and mixed with an emulsifier; then the mixture is stirred, heated, and poured into molds. Sometimes flavoring or coloring products are added. Usually treated with preservatives, processed cheeses have an almost infinite shelf life.

Some processed cheeses keep their original family name, provided they are made only from natural cheeses of that name. The most notable American-made examples of these are *processed Cheddar* and *processed Swiss*. Both U.S. and Swiss producers make a *processed Gruyère*.

Processed cheeses may also be made from two or more types of natural cheese. The most famous U.S.-made example is *American cheese*, the ubiquitous, imperishable, presliced stuff of grammar school lunchboxes. It is often made from Cheddar or one of its relatives and Swiss or one of its kin. The result is a curiously pliable, extremely mild cheese with echoes of a mild Cheddar's flavor.

A great many of the processed cheeses go by proprietary names. *Velveeta* is a well-known U.S. model. *La Vache Qui Rit* (Laughing Cow) and *Six de Savoie* are familiar examples from France of foil-wrapped little cubes or wedges of softened, Swiss-based cheese. They're creamy enough to spread. *La Grappe* is a similar cheese hiding inside a hard crust of grape seeds.

Products identified as "process cheese food" may be made not only from cheese, but from other dairy products.

GOAT'S MILK CHEESES

Chèvre is the most common of all goat cheeses, but the group also includes blues, bloomy rinds, and aged cheeses hard enough to grate. Fresh goat cheeses are primarily eating cheeses, though they are delicious in salads and omelets and are sometimes called for in other recipes such as calzone.

Buying and storing: When buying fresh chèvres, look for stark white paste and moist texture. Avoid cheeses with dried surfaces or ammoniated aromas. Among aged goat cheeses, look for smooth, pale ivory paste and smooth, uncracked rinds. Refrigerate all types in lightly waxed paper or plastic wrap.

CHÈVRE

Chèvre (French for "goat") is the generic name for goat cheeses. Chèvres are made in most parts of France, and almost all French chèvres carry a specific, usually geographic, name. Most are formed into the familiar log shape, as are *Bûcheron,* the intensely flavored *Cabicou,* and *Montrachet* (shown top). However, the curiously malleable curds of goat's milk permit this cheese to be molded into almost any shape. Among the other shapes commercially available are little balls (such as *bouton de chèvre*), thick ovals (such as *Taupinière,* shown center), and fanciful pyramids (such as *St. Chevrier,* bottom, and *Valençay*). In whatever shape, chèvres contribute inimitable textures and flavors to any cheese board. They come plain or coated with herbs, pepper, or edible vegetable ash.

A fair number of French chèvres are, in fact, part cow's milk. Included among these—often if not always—are *Banon* and *St. Marcellin.* (All-goat's-milk cheeses are marked *pur chèvre.*)

AMERICAN CHÈVRE

As a new wave of specialty cheesemaking has taken hold in the U.S., chèvre has been at the forefront; tiny producers are scattered across the country. Outstanding examples available in the West include *Cabecou, Calistogan,* and *Chèvrefeuille* (all from California and all with the curiously grainy texture so familiar from France), and *Texas Goat Cheese* (milder and creamier than the others). U.S.-made chèvres come plain (top right) and with coatings such as herbs (left), paprika (bottom right), pepper, and vegetable ash.

AMERICAN AGED GOAT CHEESE

Using various European models, American cheesemakers now produce several aged goat cheeses, including strongly flavored *Crottin* (left), patterned after France's even stronger *Crottin de Chavignol; Tome* (right), a pungent cheese that's hard enough to grate; goat's-milk *Caciota,* a firm and quite piquant cheese; and *aged goat cheese,* which, like Tome, is pungent and gratable.

GRATING CHEESES

For most people, Parmesan comes to mind first as the hard cheese that gets grated into a granular form. Italy's Parmigiano Reggiano is the original Parmesan, but there are several other *grana* types from Italy, and still more from elsewhere. Because they serve their primary purpose so well, grating cheeses often go overlooked as eating and melting types. Sliced rather than grated, all types described below make fine eating cheeses and can be used as ingredients in such dishes as pastas, omelets, and crêpes. For such purposes, they should be purchased and used before they get too dry and crumbly.

Buying and storing: If purchased for eating, these cheeses should have comparatively pale ivory paste. The darker the paste, the drier and harder the cheese. Store hard cheeses wrapped in cloth, unrefrigerated; or refrigerate them in lightly waxed paper or plastic wrap.

ASIAGO

Asiago walks a tightrope between buttery and piquant qualities. Though it's now made from cow's milk, it was originally a sheep's milk cheese—and somehow keeps the piquancy and even some of the flavors associated with such cheeses. From Alpine Italy, Asiago is often sold after only a few months' aging (*Asiago Fresco*), making it a fine, if crumbly, eating cheese. The pure grating style ages for a year or more. Both styles melt readily, whether grated or sliced.

DRY JACK

Once a prominent part of California cheesemaking, dry jack is now made by just two small dairies. If cured for no more than a year, dry jack retains enough moisture to be sliced. It also melts uncommonly well at this stage. Aged for more than a year, it may become a bit crumbly, but even then it has a welcome softness when grated. Dry jack is deliciously sweet and nutty, whether eaten alone or cooked.

KASSERI

Though still made from goat's milk in Greece, kasseri has also flowered as a U.S.-made cow's milk cheese. Many, including knowledgeable critics, prefer the American version to the original. *American kasseri* (shown in photo) is ivory to white and just hard enough to grate, with a slightly more piquant, less buttery flavor than most other grating cheeses. The Greek original is noticeably sharper than American kasseri.

PARMIGIANO REGGIANO

The true, original Parmesan cheese remains one of the most flavorful and piquant of all *grana* types. This most prestigious of grating cheeses is made only from summer milk from a legally defined region in northern and central Italy. Aged for 2 years, Parmigiano Reggiano has a rich, buttery flavor, making it a good eating cheese as well as a fine ingredient in cookery. Aged 3 years, the cheese takes on earthier, more concentrated flavors and is best used in cooking.

PECORINO

The most famous *grana*-type sheep's milk cheeses come from a legally defined part of central Italy (*Pecorino Romano*) and the island of Sardinia (*Pecorino Sardo*). Southern Italy produces huge volumes under the simple name *Pecorino*. Connoisseurs argue whether Pecorino or Parmigiano is the more flavorful, but Pecorino is certainly the more piquant—and often very salty. Grating is usually required in order for it to melt evenly.

SBRINZ

One of the oldest cheeses in the world, Sbrinz (or any Swiss mountain cheese selling as Sbrinz) defies easy classification. By taste and cheesemaking technique, it is surely Swiss—perhaps the forerunner of all cheeses now called Swiss. But it is also firm enough to be an outstanding grating cheese.

OTHER GRATING CHEESES

Italy has a number of grating cheeses aside from Parmigiano and Pecorino. Much like Parmigiano, though perhaps slightly less flavorful, is *Grana Padano* (shown in photo), often sold in the U.S. as "Parmesan" or "Parmigiano." The Argentinian *Reggianito* is also a good copy of Parmigiano. The most serious U.S. attempts at copying Parmigiano Reggiano rank behind both of these.

Agur, a sheep's milk cheese from the French Basque country, is excellent for both eating and grating. It is less salty than either Pecorino Romano or Pecorino Sardo.

U.S.-made Asiago comes close to the Italian original as an eating cheese, but it is seldom aged long enough to grate well.

THE HOLLANDERS

Holland makes many cheeses, but its best-known natives are the near twins Edam and Gouda. A third, Leyden, is gaining favor with U.S. audiences. Several other European firm cheeses are included in this section. All are primarily for eating, but several melt well.

Buying and storing: These inside-to-outside ripeners age almost imperceptibly. Refrigerate in lightly waxed paper or plastic wrap.

EDAM

Edam—the familiar red ball—comes in three forms. Plain Edam (shown) is the mildest and blandest in flavor and the softest in texture. Aged Edam, a somewhat darker gold in color, has a slightly nutty flavor. Very aged Edam, darker still, has a pronounced sweet, nutty flavor and just begins to be grainy in texture.

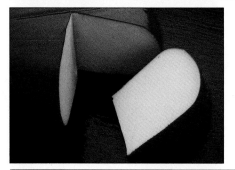

GOUDA

Gouda comes in three forms very much like Edam's. Regular Gouda (shown) is pale and slightly springy to the touch, and has a subtly nutty flavor. It may have a bit more tang than an Edam. *Farmhouse Gouda*, both tangier and more flavorful than regular Gouda, is still sweet and mild enough for anybody who likes mild Cheddar. *Mona Lisa* is the darkest and longest-aged style. Not at all piquant, it has a rich flavor not unlike browned butter.

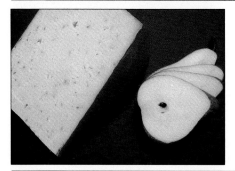

LEYDEN

Wheel-shaped Leyden cheeses would taste much like Edam and Gouda, were they not seeded with caraway, cloves, and cumin. Leydens with *Boerenkäse* printed on their gray-green rinds are farm-made. Those without that legend are factory-made and less forceful in flavor.

OTHER EUROPEAN FIRM CHEESES

France makes two firm cheeses—one quite similar to Edam, the other truly original. The Edam-like cheese is called *Mimolette* (bottom left); it even comes in a round ball. *Cantal* (top and right) has been made in Normandy for at least 2,000 years; it's quite robust in flavor as firm cheeses go. A smaller, pasteurized version called *Cantelet* is also available. Italy's firm cheese is *Friulano*.

JACK CHEESES

Jack is a Californian semisoft cheese, sometimes sold as Monterey jack. (Dry jack is distantly related; see pages 7 and 22.)

Buying and storing: Made moist and sold young, jack keeps well for weeks, growing slightly softer with age. Refrigerate in lightly waxed paper or plastic wrap.

THE JACKS

Monterey jack and just *jack* are the same basic cheese: moist, pliable, and among the mildest flavored of all cheeses. Its gentle flavor and readiness to melt make jack so versatile in cooking that it is recommended in many of the recipes in this book. The same mildness causes producers to flavor it with everything from garlic to chiles. Flavored or plain, it makes a fine sandwich cheese.

STORING CHEESE

Every cheese benefits by being refrigerated, with the possible exception of a Brie or Camembert being hurried to ripeness for tomorrow's dinner. Only the hardest grating cheeses can be safely left out in a cool room—and then only if lightly wrapped in cheesecloth, *not* in wax paper or plastic wrap (they will grow moldy if surface moisture cannot escape).

Clear plastic wrap is a suitable wrapping for refrigerated cheeses. However, some cheese fanciers strongly prefer lightly waxed paper—the cut squares like butchers use, not the heavily waxed translucent type sold in rolls. These connoisseurs argue that plastic either taints fine cheeses or is so airtight that it causes them to develop or concentrate undesirable aromas of their own.

Avoid wrapping cheeses in foil, even if you purchased the cheese in a foil wrapper. Foils come in many different types; some kinds interact with the acids in cheese, altering the flavor.

Store very strong cheeses (Münster, Limburger, etc.) in airtight plastic containers after wrapping them in wax paper or plastic wrap. This two-layer packaging will prevent the cheeses from aromatizing everything in the refrigerator.

Freezing is a less-than-perfect solution to long-term cheese storage. It would certainly be convenient if soft-ripened cheeses could be frozen successfully (because of their short life spans), but these are the very types that are most likely to lose flavor and change in texture. Firm or hard cheeses are better candidates for freezing, but even with these, some change in flavor and/or texture is likely. Any cheese bound for the freezer should be wrapped in freezer paper and tightly sealed. And remember that, in general, the shorter the freeze, the better.

MONASTERY CHEESES . . . & BEYOND

This is a broad group of mildly to powerfully aromatic, ripened semisoft cheeses. Many in the group are called "monastery" cheeses, since the techniques used to make them were developed in European monasteries. Technically, most are brushed-rind or washed-rind cheeses. These curing techniques keep the surfaces moist and warm, which is to say hospitable to flavoring bacteria. Aroma concentrates in the rind, leaving the paste relatively mild. Die-hard connoisseurs insist that one has not eaten the cheese unless the rind is eaten, too, but newcomers will usually prefer to cut the rind away. All these cheeses are primarily eating cheeses, though adventuresome cooks might use them—selectively—for a bold change of pace in omelets and soufflés.

Buying and storing: Properly ripe semisoft cheeses never ooze, but become so soft they cling to the knife when sliced. They ripen, then overripen, within weeks. Avoid slimy or hardened and cracked rinds. Refrigerate in lightly waxed paper or plastic wrap; store wrapped cheeses in sealed plastic containers to avoid tainting other foods.

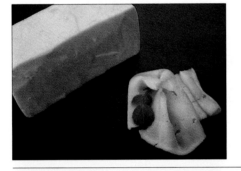

BEER CHEESE

Not a monastery cheese, but a washed rind nonetheless, Beer Cheese originated in Germany and came to the United States with German-speaking immigrants. Milky white inside and out, often with small holes dotting the paste, Beer Cheese smells more pungent than it tastes. In terms of intensity of flavor, it falls about in the middle of this group. The German originals (often labeled *Weisslacker Bierkäse*) are often a little stronger than American Beer Cheese.

BEL PAESE

Indirectly inspired by St. Paulin (see "Other Monastery Types" on page 28), Bel Paese has the texture of monastery cheeses, but only the beginnings of their flavor. The Italian original and its American descendant are hard to tell apart side by side, let alone separately. Mild flavor and rich texture make both fine on cheese boards; they also melt so well they can substitute for mozzarella in pizza.

ESROM

A Danish cheese modeled on Port du Salut (see page 28), Esrom starts mild enough but develops a pungent aroma—along with a dark orange rind and ivory paste—as it ripens. Despite its aroma, it has a sweeter quality than Beer Cheese or Limburger (see facing page). This mildness recommends it to many who do not care for the sharper washed-rind cheeses.

HAVARTI

Denmark's Havarti bridges the gap between Bel Paese and Port du Salut (see page 28) and is also a milder echo of its Danish cousin, Esrom. Most connoisseurs seeking a mild semisoft dessert cheese favor it over the German Tilsits currently available. Havarti can be found plain or flavored with caraway, dill, or chives.

LIMBURGER

The cheese that won washed rinds their American reputation for powerful aromas continues to earn its fame. Like most of these cheeses, it has its origins in German-speaking Europe, but an amply pungent American edition is made in Wisconsin. Both European and American Limburgers have stark white, solid paste inside a thin, moist, pale tan rind. Both are quite piquant, even sharp.

MÜNSTER

Alsatian Münster (shown) is described as "mild" in France and "pungent" in the U.S.—because it is eaten very young there, but almost always fully ripe here. At full tilt, it joins Esrom as the perfect demonstration of Saul Bellow's cheerful—and scientifically accurate—description of monastery types as "foot smelling cheeses." This may not sound delicious, but the cheese is. *American Münster* is a different, very bland cheese.

OKA

Canada's great monastery type has begun to appear regularly in U.S. markets. Its red-orange rind, pale ivory paste, and uncompromising aroma place it among the best in its family, a very near relative to Alsatian Münster and Esrom.

PONT L'ÉVÊQUE

Made in Normandy, not far from the town of Camembert, Pont l'Évêque is one of the earliest of the monastery cheeses and also one of those the French call great (they rank it fourth, after Brie, Camembert, and Roquefort). The flavor is usually described as indescribable . . . strong but not offensive, rich but not sharp, tangy but not bitter. Pont l'Évêque has never been imitated; in fact, the bacteria that flavor it will not transplant from certain Norman cellar walls.

(Continued on next page)

PORT DU SALUT

Just how France's Port du Salut (or *Port Salut*) differs in flavor from Pont l'Évêque (see page 27) is at least as hard to describe as how Pont l'Évêque tastes in the first place, but differ it does. Different bacteria and a different technique make it less piquant, less tangy, less pungently aromatic than Pont l'Évêque—but stronger in each of these departments than Havarti.

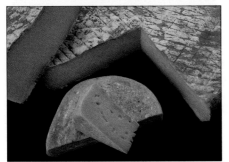

OTHER MONASTERY TYPES

St. Paulin is a very close French copy of Port du Salut. Other French washed- or brushed-rind cheeses in the monastery style include *Beaumont, Providence, Reblochon* (bottom), *St. Nectaire* (top), and *Tomme de Savoie*. Reblochon, in particular, has a fine reputation. German *Tilsit* is a blander semisoft cheese with little or no pungency in flavor or aroma.

OTHER STRONG WASHED RINDS

Schloss (shown), California's entry in the strong cheese sweepstakes, can be bought fresh, so it may be quite mild. But if it is not strong enough to start with, it will get there. The other three strong cheeses made in the U.S.—*brick, hand*, and *Liederkrantz*—can be hard to find. France makes two rarely imported powerhouses called *Livarot* and *Maroilles*. Maroilles can be so pungent that one connoisseur advises scraping the rind off outdoors before bringing the cheese to the table.

STRACCHINO CHEESES

Connoisseurs debate about what Stracchino is. The name means "tired milk" in local Italian dialect, and it once referred to all Lombard cheeses made as cows moved from summer to winter pasture. This is no longer the case. The name now covers many mild, semisoft Italian cheeses.

Buying and storing: Stracchino cheeses should be moist and only mildly aromatic. Refrigerate in lightly waxed paper or plastic wrap.

CRESCENZA & TALEGGIO

Crescenza is sold very young (often within 10 days of manufacture), when it is so mild and spreadable that it often substitutes for butter in its home country. Italian Crescenza is hard to export in prime condition, but a Texas specialist makes a fine one. Taleggio (shown), a fine eating cheese, is not as mild as Crescenza. The longer-aged *Taleggio di monte* acquires such definite flavors that it resembles some of the milder monastery cheeses.

STRING CHEESES

String cheeses—*pasta filatas* in Italy, where they are common—are mild-flavored and great for cooking; we would not have pizza without them. They also make pleasing, chewy snacks. Fresh or aged, they come by their elastic properties because the curd is kneaded and stretched as it forms.

Buying and storing: All the string cheeses except provolone are meant to be bought young, for immediate consumption. Look for springy texture and pale paste. Refrigerate in lightly waxed paper or plastic wrap.

CACIOCAVALLO

The mildly piquant *Caciocavallo* (or *Cacio a cavallo*) does not get as stringy when cooked as most of its kin, but rather gets chewier. An Italian import, it has an especially memorable flavor when cut in bite-sized chunks and fried in oil, garlic, and herbs as an appetizer. The name can be loosely translated as "cheese on horseback," after the way the cheese is hung up for aging.

MOZZARELLA

When fresh, mozzarellas are softer than even cottage cheese, silky smooth, and amazingly delicate to the taste. Italians eat them at this point, often with sliced fresh tomatoes and basil. The finest, most flavorful Italian mozzarellas are made from water buffalo's milk and carry the name *mozzarella di bufala*. Good ones are also made from cow's milk. Mozzarella is available both smoked (left) and fresh (right).

AMERICAN MOZZARELLA

A few small specialty producers in the U.S. make mozzarella just the way it is done in Rome, with memorably similar results. "Supermarket mozzarella" is a different cheese. Less moist and thus much more rubbery, it is not much as an eating cheese, but does yeoman service as the stringy cheese that makes pizza such an arm-waving adventure to eat.

PROVOLONE

In effect aged mozzarella, provolone is primarily a cooking cheese. *Dolce*, the common import to the U.S., is the milder form; *piccante* is sharper, crumblier, and more flavorful. Dolce ages for a few months, piccante for up to 2 years. Some provolone is smoked to add flavor. The cheese comes in many shapes and in all sizes, from a few ounces to 200 pounds, every one hand-molded. The Italian original has a metal tab on top.

(Continued on next page)

OTHER STRING CHEESES

The generic *American string cheese* (left) has a very mild to outright bland flavor, and the happy characteristic of splitting into "strings" of any size for chewing as a snack. Its straight, sticklike shape makes splitting easy. *Armenian braided cheese* (right), also bland, is chewier—more like Caciocavallo.

SWISS CHEESES

Gentle-flavored, meltable, and easily sliced, the Swiss family of cheeses lends itself to scores of uses in cooking, and makes for great eating as well. The identifying marks are holes ("eyes") created by a gas that forms as the cheese ripens. The characteristic flavor comes from the same source.

Buying and storing: Cheeses in perfect condition show an evenly colored paste and a moist sheen in the eyes. Overaged cheeses have cracks in their brownish rinds and a dried, sandy texture. Refrigerate in lightly waxed paper or plastic wrap.

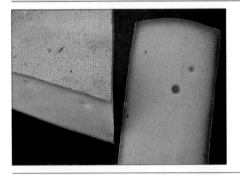

APPENZELLER

Less familiar to Americans than Gruyère or Emmenthaler (the other true "Swisses"), Appenzeller differs from its illustrious kinfolk in that it is made from unpasteurized milk and soaked for several days in a wine or cider bath. It has a higher moisture content and a milder flavor than either Emmenthaler or Gruyère. Appenzeller sold in the U.S. is usually somewhat more piquant and flavorful than that found in Europe, since it is aged longer.

EMMENTHALER

The most exported of the true Swiss cheeses is also the one the Swiss think most difficult to make, because, at its best, it preserves most clearly the original flavors of the milk used in its production. Made in wheels weighing as much as 220 pounds, most Emmenthalers exported to the U.S. cure for as little as 4 months—compared to 10 months for cheeses exported to many parts of Europe, where stronger flavors are preferred. Emmenthalers have many large eyes.

GRUYÈRE

The fondue cheese of choice for many, Gruyère has the sweetest, nuttiest flavor of the true Swiss cheeses, and it's the firmest of the famous ones. It ages for the same time as Emmenthaler, but is made in smaller wheels (around 80 pounds) and has fewer, smaller eyes.

RACLETTE

Raclettes are a whole family of cheeses from the canton of Valais. They taste much like Gruyère. While they are tasty dessert cheeses, they are even more prized for use in the dish with which they share a name (see page 73). The French pan-fry their raclette rather than melt it before a fire or on a special toaster.

AMERICAN SWISSES

Swiss immigrants launched cheesemaking in Wisconsin; their descendants still dominate the dairies there, where a few specialists continue to make outstanding Swiss-type cheeses using all the traditional techniques. Deep ivory colors, firm paste, and definite flavors separate these cheeses from the blander, moister mass-produced types.

DENMARK'S "BO" CHEESES

Samsoe (bottom left) and all the "bos"—*Danbo, Elbo, Fynbo, Maribo, Molbo, Svenbo,* and *Tybo* (top and right) are made in the Swiss way. They resemble one or another of the Swiss cheeses—and each other—in both texture and flavor.

THE FRENCH CONNECTION

France, not surprisingly, makes excellent Swiss-style cheeses; some are made just across the border, others farther away. *Comte* (left) resembles Emmenthaler, but since it's sometimes aged longer, it may be more flavorful than the Emmanthalers exported to the United States. *Goutu* (right) bridges the narrow gap between Appenzeller and Emmenthaler. *Beaufort* (hard to find) comes close to Gruyère.

OTHER EUROPEAN SWISSES

Steady, reliable Norwegian *Jarlsberg* (shown) looks like a Swiss cheese but, to the most discerning palate, does not taste quite like any of them. Both Jarlsberg and *Vallio*, a Finnish Swiss, have sweet, mild flavors that make them versatile substitutes for Swiss. The same is true of Bavarian *Alpentop* and Austrian *Steiermark.*

COOKING WITH CHEESE

When people think of cooking with cheese, the big four come to mind at once—cream, Cheddar, Swiss, and Parmesan. There is reason behind their popularity: cream, Cheddar, and Swiss lend themselves to many roles, thanks both to their textures and their appealing flavors. Even if Parmesan is not quite as versatile, there is more to do with it than sprinkle it on top of pasta.

But what to do with Asiago, Brie, and all the others? Substitute them for Swiss, Cheddar, cream, or Parmesan. The job is easier if one member of a family is substituted for another, because—in general—members of a family behave similarly. But crossing family lines takes only a little extra thought.

The cheeses that can go into hot soups, for example, must melt smoothly without becoming too stringy. Swiss is about the limit—ask someone who has tried mozzarella in a hot broth! More restrictions apply to cheeses that go into sweet desserts. Usually, only the mild-flavored fresh types will do. Most of the flavorful ripened cheeses are far from sweet. Though they're desserts in themselves in the European tradition, they're not something to fold into a cheese and berry pie.

Though there are other dishes or groups of dishes with limited adaptability, many of the most familiar cheese dishes allow almost free choice. Take the omelet, for example. Everybody has had Cheddar or Swiss in more than one omelet, but how about Brie, one of the blue cheeses, or Limburger? Any untried cheese can rekindle interest in what may have become an over-familiar dish. What is true of the omelet can also be true of crêpes, soufflés, and pasta.

Blending two, three, even four cheeses within a single dish is also rewarding. The Italians are masters at this simple method for building new, interesting flavors into a much-used recipe. The other advantage of blending, of course, is in the ability to tone down flavors that may be a bit too strong. Combining a mild, fresh cheese with a powerfully aromatic type lets the cook enjoy the best of both worlds.

Choose a filling of Swiss cheese
with bacon and mushrooms, or jack cheese with
ham and green chiles for these two-bite-size
Mini-Quiches (page 45). The recipe
makes a generous six dozen nibbles.

APPETIZERS

In all their variety, appetizers offer an ideal way to give new cheeses a tryout—or to show old favorites in new lights. Almost every cheese can serve as party fare or help get a meal underway.

◆ BAKED BRIE IN CRUST ◆

Brie or any other "bloomy rind" cheese baked in a hollowed-out French loaf makes a creamy appetizer for a party. Scaled down and served with a green salad, it makes a satisfying dinner for two to four.

      1 round or oval loaf (1½ lbs.) French bread
      ⅓ cup olive oil or melted butter or
         margarine
      2 cloves garlic, minced or pressed
      1 to 1½ pounds Brie, Camembert, or St.
         André cheese

Using a serrated knife and your fingers, remove center of bread in a single piece, leaving a shell about ½ inch thick on sides and bottom. Around rim of bread shell, make 1½-inch-deep cuts about 1½ inches apart. Cut removed bread into 1½- by 2-inch chunks about ½ inch thick.

Mix oil and garlic. Brush inside of shell with about 3 tablespoons of the garlic oil; brush bread chunks with remaining oil. Trim rind from cheese, if desired. Cut or tear cheese into chunks; place in bread shell.

Place filled shell and bread chunks in a single layer on two 10- by 15-inch baking sheets. Bake in a 350° oven for about 15 minutes. Remove bread chunks to a rack; let cool. Continue to bake filled shell until cut edges are golden and cheese is melted (about 10 more minutes).

Place filled shell on a serving board; surround with toasted bread chunks. To eat, dip toasted bread chunks and crisp pieces from edges of bread shell into melted cheese. Makes 10 to 12 servings.

CHEESE IN CRUST FOR TWO TO FOUR

Follow directions for **Baked Brie in Crust,** but use 1 small round or oval loaf (about ⅓ lb.) French bread; 8 ounces Brie, Camembert, or St. André cheese; 3 tablespoons olive oil or melted butter or margarine; and 1 clove garlic, minced or pressed.

◆ ALMOND-CHEDDAR BALL ◆

Cream cheese and sherry temper the sharpness of Cheddar in this smooth spread. A coating of toasted almonds adds sweetness and crunch.

      2 cups (8 oz.) shredded sharp Cheddar
         cheese
      4 ounces cream cheese, cut into chunks
         and softened
      1 tablespoon *each* dry sherry and
         mayonnaise
     1½ teaspoons Dijon mustard
         Dash of ground red pepper (cayenne)
      3 tablespoons finely chopped sweet pickle
      ⅓ cup coarsely chopped blanched almonds
         Crackers

In large bowl of an electric mixer, combine Cheddar cheese, cream cheese, sherry, mayonnaise, mustard, and red pepper. Beat until smooth and well blended. Stir in pickle. Cover and refrigerate until firm. Shape into a ball, wrap in plastic wrap, and refrigerate for at least 2 hours or up to 2 weeks.

Meanwhile, spread almonds in a shallow baking pan; bake in a 350° oven until golden (about 8 minutes). Let cool.

To serve, roll chilled cheese ball in almonds to coat; let stand at room temperature for 1½ to 2 hours. Accompany with crackers. Makes 3 cups.

◆ BRANDIED BLUE CHEESE SPREAD ◆

Both brandy and blue cheese add definite flavors to this creamy spread.

      3 ounces blue-veined cheese
      2 tablespoons butter or margarine,
         softened
      1 small package (3 oz.) cream cheese,
         softened
      2 tablespoons brandy
         Red or Golden Delicious apple wedges,
         celery stalks, or unsalted crackers

In small bowl of an electric mixer or in a food processor, combine blue cheese, butter, cream cheese, and brandy. Beat until smooth and well blended. Cover and refrigerate until next day. Let stand at room temperature for about 1 hour before serving. Spread on apple wedges. Makes about 1 cup.

Two mild cheeses play off against a zesty green chile dip
in Salsa Potato Skins (page 44). Served hot from the broiler, these popular
appetizers make perfect summer company for ice-cold lager beer.

◆ STUFFED GOUDA CHEESE ◆

Enjoy the sweet, nutty flavor of Gouda in spreadable form with this recipe.

> 1 whole baby Gouda cheese (about 14 oz.)
> ½ cup beer
> 1 teaspoon Dijon mustard
> ⅛ teaspoon ground nutmeg
> ¼ cup butter or margarine, cut into chunks and softened
> ½ teaspoon caraway seeds
> Pumpernickel bread or crackers

Cut out a circle from center top of cheese. Carefully scoop out cheese inside, leaving shell intact. Use a curved small knife, such as a grapefruit knife, to remove cheese at first; finish the job with a small spoon, scooping carefully to avoid puncturing shell.

Place ¼ cup of the beer in a food processor or blender. Cut larger pieces of removed cheese into cubes; then add all removed cheese to food processor with mustard, nutmeg, and butter. Whirl until smooth, gradually adding remaining ¼ cup beer with motor running; stir down sides of work bowl with a spatula occasionally. Stir in caraway seeds. Spoon cheese mixture into shell. (Not all of the mixture will fit; refill shell as necessary.) If made ahead, cover and refrigerate for up to 24 hours; let stand at room temperature for abour 1 hour before serving. Accompany with pumpernickel. Makes about 1½ cups.

◆ PECAN-CROWNED BAKED BRIE ◆

Choose juicy fruit wedges or crisp breadsticks for scooping up melted Brie and toasted nuts.

> 1 whole, firm Brie cheese (2 lbs.)
> 2 tablespoons butter or margarine, melted
> 1 cup pecan or walnut halves
> Apple or pear wedges or breadsticks

Place cheese in a 10- to 11-inch round rimmed baking dish (one you can bring to the table). Brush cheese with butter. Arrange pecan halves on top. Bake in a 350° oven just until cheese begins to melt (10 to 12 minutes). Keep hot on a warming tray. Serve with fruit wedges for scooping up cheese. Makes 24 servings.

◆ SAUTÉED CAMEMBERT ◆

All of the soft-ripened, or "bloomy rind," cheeses (see pages 14 and 15) take well to a bit of heat and a coating of delicate herbs and crisp crumbs.

> 1 whole, firm Camembert or Brie cheese (about 8 oz.)
> ⅓ cup fine dry bread crumbs
> ½ teaspoon fines herbes or thyme leaves
> 1 egg
> 3 tablespoons butter or margarine
> 3 tablespoons thinly sliced green onions (including tops)
> Sliced French bread, toasted

Let cheese stand at room temperature for about 15 minutes. Mix bread crumbs and fines herbes in a shallow dish. In another shallow dish, beat egg. Coat cheese in egg, then in crumb mixture.

Melt butter in a small frying pan over medium-low heat. Add cheese and cook until golden on bottom (1 to 2 minutes), then turn. (If cheese begins to leak at edges before bottom is golden, turn immediately.) Cook until lightly browned on other side (½ to 1 minute). If desired, transfer to a warm plate. Garnish with onions and serve hot, with French bread. Makes 4 to 6 servings.

◆ GARLIC-HERB CHEESE ◆

Garlic and herbs make a cream cheese spread that's reminiscent of the French *Boursin* (see page 19).

> 1 large package (8 oz.) cream cheese, softened
> 3 tablespoons lemon juice
> ½ teaspoon dry or 1 teaspoon fresh winter or summer savory leaves
> ¼ to ½ teaspoon freshly ground black pepper
> 1 clove garlic, minced or pressed
> Whipping cream or milk
> Crackers or melba toast

In small bowl of an electric mixer, beat cream cheese until smooth. Beat in lemon juice, savory, pepper, and garlic. If mixture is too thick, beat in a little cream. Mound in a small bowl or press into a greased 1½-cup mold. Cover and refrigerate for at least 2 hours or up to 2 days. Let stand at room temperature for 30 minutes before serving. Accompany with crackers. Makes about 1¼ cups.

BOTTOMLESS CHEESE CROCK

Once the crock gets going, add firm cheeses and a moistener (see recipe) at any time to replenish it.

- 4 cups (l lb.) shredded sharp Cheddar cheese, at room temperature
- 1 small package (3 oz.) cream cheese, softened
- 1 to 2 tablespoons olive oil
- 1 teaspoon *each* dry mustard and garlic salt
- 2 tablespoons brandy
  Crackers

In large bowl of an electric mixer, combine Cheddar cheese, cream cheese, oil, mustard, garlic salt, and brandy. Beat until well blended. Pack into a container, cover, and refrigerate for 1 week before using. Let stand at room temperature for about 1 hour before serving. Accompany with crackers.

After using, replenish remainder of original mixture in crock with fresh cheese as directed below to keep crock going. Makes about 3 cups.

Adding to the crock. Use firm cheeses, such as Swiss, Jack, or Cheddar. Shred cheese and beat in, adding small amounts of olive oil or cream cheese for good consistency. Add 1½ teaspoons brandy, sherry, port, beer, or kirsch for each cup of cheese added. After adding fresh cheese, cover and refrigerate for at least several days before serving.

◆ STUFFED CAMEMBERT ◆

Blending turns four cheeses—three of them distinctively flavored—into a singular spread.

- 1 whole, medium-ripe Camembert cheese (about 8 oz.)
- 1 wedge (1¼ oz.) Roquefort or other blue-veined cheese, crumbled
- 1 cup (4 oz.) shredded Cheddar cheese
- 1 small package (3 oz.) cream cheese, cut into chunks
- 1 small clove garlic, minced or pressed
- 1 teaspoon Italian herb seasoning
- 1 tablespoon chopped parsley
- 2 tablespoons butter or margarine, softened
- ¼ cup thinly sliced green onions (including tops)
  Crackers or melba toast

Refrigerate Camembert until very cold (2 to 3 hours). With a sharp knife, cut around top, about ¼ inch in from edge, cutting down about ½ inch into cheese. Then carefully scoop out cheese (including top rind) with a spoon, leaving a ¼-inch-thick shell. Wrap shell and refrigerate.

Place removed Camembert, Roquefort, Cheddar, and cream cheeses in large bowl of an electric mixer. Let stand at room temperature until softened, then beat until smooth and creamy. Beat in garlic, herb seasoning, parsley, and butter; stir in onions. Mound cheese mixture in Camembert shell. Cover and refrigerate for at least 24 hours or up to 4 days. Let stand at room temperature for 1 hour before serving. Accompany with crackers. Makes about 2 cups.

◆ GORGONZOLA CHEESE TORTA ◆

This simple appetizer is no more than alternating layers of cream cheese and Gorgonzola. Serve it as a spread for plain crackers, with fruit alongside.

- 1 large package (8 oz.) cream cheese, softened
- 1 cup (½ lb.) unsalted butter, softened
- 12 ounces Gorgonzola or other blue-veined cheese
  Crackers and sliced ripe pears or whole grapes

In large bowl of an electric mixer, beat cream cheese and butter until very smoothly blended. Set aside. Using your fingers, finely crumble Gorgonzola cheese; set aside.

Cut two 18-inch squares of cheesecloth (or an 18-inch square of unbleached muslin); moisten with water, wring dry, and lay out flat, one on top of the other. Use cloth to smoothly line a 4- to 5-cup straight-sided plain mold such as a charlotte mold, loaf pan, terrine, or clean flowerpot; drape excess cloth over rim of mold.

Place ⅓ of the Gorgonzola in an even layer in mold bottom. Top with ⅓ of the cream cheese mixture and spread evenly. Repeat layers until mold is filled, ending with cream cheese mixture.

Fold ends of cloth over top and press down lightly with your hands to compact. Refrigerate until torta feels firm when pressed (about 1 hour) or for up to 5 days.

To serve, grasp ends of cloth and lift torta from mold. Invert torta onto a serving dish and gently pull off cloth. Accompany with crackers and fruit. Makes 16 to 18 servings.

Cheddar adds distinctive flavor to many forms of bread, including these savory
baked appetizers. Clockwise from the top are Cheese Herb Pretzels,
Cheese Twists, Cheese Spritz, and Sesame Cheese Wafers. Recipes are on the facing page.

◆ CHEESE HERB PRETZELS ◆

Pictured on facing page

Flaky, light cheese pretzels can stand alone as a snack or replace crackers when served with soup.

- 1 **cup all-purpose flour**
- 2 **tablespoons grated Parmesan cheese**
- ½ **teaspoon garlic powder**
- ¼ **teaspoon** *each* **dry basil, dry rosemary, and oregano leaves**
- ½ **cup (¼ lb.) firm butter or margarine**
- 1 **cup (4 oz.) shredded sharp Cheddar cheese**
- 2 **to 3 tablespoons cold water**

In a large bowl, stir together flour, Parmesan cheese, garlic powder, basil, rosemary, and oregano. Using a pastry blender or 2 knives, cut in butter until mixture resembles fine crumbs. Stir in Cheddar cheese.

Sprinkle water over flour mixture, 1 tablespoon at a time, stirring lightly with a fork until dough holds together. Gather dough into a ball with your hands. Divide dough in half, then cut each half into 12 equal pieces. (If dough is soft, wrap in plastic wrap and refrigerate until firm.)

Place each piece of dough on a lightly floured board; roll back and forth with your palms to make an 11-inch strand. Twist each strand into a pretzel shape. Place pretzels slightly apart on ungreased baking sheets. Bake in a 425° oven until golden brown (12 to 15 minutes). Let cool on racks.

If made ahead, package airtight and freeze for up to a month. To recrisp, place frozen pretzels on baking sheets and heat in a 350° oven for 5 to 7 minutes. Makes 2 dozen appetizers.

CHEESE TWISTS

Pictured on facing page

Prepare dough as directed for **Cheese Herb Pretzels,** but omit Parmesan cheese, garlic powder, basil, rosemary, and oregano. Instead, mix flour with ½ teaspoon *each* **salt** and **ground ginger.** Decrease butter or margarine to ⅓ cup; add ½ teaspoon **Worcestershire** to cold water.

To shape dough, on a lightly floured board, roll dough out to a 10-inch square. Lightly beat 1 **egg;** brush over dough. Sprinkle dough evenly with 2 tablespoons **sesame, caraway, or poppy seeds** or coarse salt. Cut dough square in half; cut each half into ½-inch-wide, 5-inch-long strips. Hold each strip at both ends and twist in opposite directions.

Place twists 1 inch apart on greased baking sheets. Bake in a 400° oven until golden brown (10 to 12 minutes). Serve warm. Or let cool on racks; serve at room temperature. Makes 40 appetizers.

◆ CHEESE SPRITZ ◆

Pictured on facing page

Sharp Cheddar offers a counterpoint to the flavors of sesame or poppy seeds. You can shape the dough into pressed "cookies" or wafers, then freeze for later use.

- ⅔ **cup butter or margarine, softened**
- ½ **cup shredded sharp Cheddar cheese**
- 1 **egg**
- ⅛ **teaspoon ground red pepper (cayenne)**
- ¼ **teaspoon dry mustard**
- ½ **teaspoon** *each* **salt and sugar**
- 1⅔ **cups all-purpose flour**
- **Poppy or sesame seeds**

In large bowl of an electric mixer, beat together butter and cheese. Add egg, red pepper, mustard, salt, and sugar; beat until well blended. Gradually add flour, stirring until smoothly blended. Shape dough into a ball with your hands.

Firmly pack dough into a cookie press fitted with a star plate. Shape cookies on ungreased baking sheets, spacing them about 1 inch apart. Sprinkle with poppy seeds. Bake in a 375° oven until lightly browned (10 to 12 minutes). Serve warm; or let cool on racks and serve at room temperature.

If made ahead, package airtight and freeze for up to a month. Makes about 2½ dozen appetizers.

SESAME CHEESE WAFERS

Pictured on facing page

Prepare dough as directed for **Cheese Spritz.** Divide dough in half and shape each portion into a smooth log about 1½ inches in diameter. For each portion, sprinkle 1½ tablespoons **sesame seeds** on a sheet of wax paper or plastic wrap. Roll log in seeds to coat evenly, pressing lightly to embed seeds in dough. Wrap log in wax paper or plastic wrap and refrigerate until firm enough to slice easily (at least 2 hours) or for up to 24 hours.

Slice dough about ¼ inch thick and arrange slices slightly apart on ungreased baking sheets. Bake in a 375° oven until wafers are golden on bottom and just firm when lightly touched (10 to 12 minutes). Serve warm; or let cool on racks and serve at room temperature.

If made ahead, package airtight and freeze for up to a month. Makes about 5 dozen appetizers.

◆ LAYERED CHEESE TORTA WITH PESTO ◆

Layers of mascarpone (see page 20) and a colorful filling add up to Italian *torta*, a simple but impressive-looking spread for bread, crackers, or vegetables. Because mascarpone isn't always easy to find, we've used cream cheese and unsalted butter in its place.

3 large packages (8 oz. *each*) cream cheese, softened
3 cups (1½ lbs.) unsalted butter, softened
Pesto Filling (recipe follows)
Basil sprig
Thinly sliced French bread
Assorted crisp raw vegetables

In large bowl of an electric mixer, beat cream cheese and butter until very smoothly blended, scraping mixture from sides of bowl as needed.

Prepare Pesto Filling and set aside.

Cut two 18-inch squares of cheesecloth (or an 18-inch square of unbleached muslin); moisten with water, wring dry, and lay out flat, one on top of the other. Use cloth to smoothly line a 10-cup straight-sided plain mold such as a tall brioche or charlotte mold, a loaf pan, or a clean flowerpot; drape excess cloth over rim of mold.

With your fingers or a rubber spatula, spread ⅛ of the cheese mixture in prepared mold. Cover with ⅐ of the filling, extending it evenly to sides of mold. Repeat layers until mold is filled, finishing with cheese. (If you prefer thinner or thicker layers, divide cheese and filling accordingly, but always use cheese for bottom and top layers.)

Fold ends of cloth over top and press down lightly with your hands to compact. Refrigerate until torta feels firm when pressed (1 to 1½ hours). Grasp ends of cloth and lift torta from mold. Invert onto a serving dish and gently pull off cloth; if allowed to stay on cheese longer than about 1½ hours, cloth will act as a wick and cause filling color to bleed onto cheese.

If made ahead, cover with plastic wrap and refrigerate for up to 5 days. Garnish with basil sprig just before serving; offer with bread and vegetables. Makes 20 to 25 servings.

Pesto Filling. In a food processor or blender, whirl to a paste 3¼ cups lightly packed **fresh basil leaves,** 1½ cups (about 7½ oz.) freshly grated **Parmesan or Romano cheese,** and ½ cup **olive oil.** Stir in 6 tablespoons **pine nuts** and season to taste with **salt** and **pepper.**

◆ CHEESE RAMEKINS ◆

These ramekins offer an extra generous serving of cheese melted on toast. Have them assembled, ready to bake, for brunch, lunch, or after the theater.

6 to 8 slices firm-textured white bread
½ cup (¼ lb.) butter or margarine
3 to 4 cups (¾ to 1 lb.) shredded fontina, provolone, or jack cheese
2 tablespoons minced parsley

Select 6 to 8 shallow ½- to ¾-cup casseroles. Cut bread slices to fit into bottom of each dish. (Reserve bread trimmings for other uses, if desired.) Remove bread from casseroles; place directly on oven rack and bake in a 200° oven for 45 minutes. Turn off oven and leave toast in closed oven for 1 hour.

Melt butter in a wide frying pan over low heat. Add toast and cook, turning as needed, until golden brown on both sides. Place a toast slice in each casserole. Distribute cheese evenly over toast. (At this point, you may cover and refrigerate until next day.)

Sprinkle with parsley. Bake, uncovered, in a 400° oven until cheese is bubbling (5 to 8 minutes). Makes 6 to 8 servings.

◆ POLENTA DIAMONDS ◆

Two classics from Italy—polenta and Gorgonzola—work together in these savory, easy-to-make appetizers.

2 tablespoons butter or margarine
1 medium-size onion, finely chopped
5½ cups regular-strength chicken broth
1¾ cups polenta (Italian-style cornmeal) or yellow cornmeal
8 to 12 ounces Gorgonzola cheese

Melt butter in a 4- to 5-quart pan over medium-high heat. Add onion and cook, stirring often, until onion just begins to brown (about 7 minutes). Add 4 cups of the broth. Cover, increase heat to high, and bring to a boil.

In a medium bowl, stir together polenta and remaining 1½ cups broth. Using a long-handled spoon, stir polenta mixture into boiling broth. Cook, stirring, until thickened; mixture spatters and is very hot, so be careful. Reduce heat to low.

Continue to cook, stirring, until polenta is stiff enough to hold its shape for about 10 seconds after spoon is drawn across pan bottom (15 to 20 minutes). At once pour into a buttered 10- by 15-inch rimmed baking pan and quickly spread out to make an even layer.

Cut cheese into ¼-inch-thick sticks. Arrange cheese sticks in parallel 15-inch-long rows about 1 inch apart on polenta, pressing cheese partway into polenta. Let polenta cool. Using a long knife, cut through polenta between rows of cheese to make strips about 1 inch wide. Cut across strips diagonally at 1-inch intervals to make diamond shapes. (At this point, you may cover and refrigerate for up to 2 days. Bring to room temperature before continuing.)

To serve, broil polenta (still in pan) 6 inches below heat until cheese is sizzling (about 5 minutes). If necessary, run a knife along existing cuts to separate pieces. With a wide spatula, transfer pieces to a tray. Serve hot or at room temperature. Makes about 8 dozen appetizers.

FILA CAMEO APPETIZERS

Fila and goat cheese both contribute a Middle Eastern air to these tasty tidbits.

> **Goat Cheese Filling (recipe follows)**
> **About ½ cup (¼ lb.) butter or margarine, melted**
> 18 **sheets fila pastry, thawed if frozen**

Prepare Goat Cheese Filling and set aside.

Brush two 12- by 15-inch baking sheets with butter. Lay one fila sheet out flat on a flat surface; keep remaining fila sheets covered with plastic wrap to prevent drying. Cut sheet in half crosswise. Lightly brush each piece with butter, then fold in half lengthwise to make a rectangle about 4 by 11 inches. Brush each rectangle with butter.

Shape each rectangle as follows. Place a chopstick along folded edge of rectangle. Holding fila against chopstick, roll pastry loosely and smoothly around chopstick to within ½ inch of opposite (cut) edge. Gently push both ends of fila on chopstick toward center until pastry is gathered into a roll about 3½ inches long. Holding gathered pastry in place, gently pull out chopstick. Curve gathered roll, free edge toward center, to make a circle, butting ends together.

Set fila "cups" on buttered baking sheet; brush lightly with butter. Cut and shape remaining fila in

the same way, making a total of 36 cups. Bake in a 350° oven until pastry is lightly browned (about 15 minutes). If made ahead, let cool on baking sheets, then wrap airtight and store at room temperature for up to 4 days.

To complete, spoon Goat Cheese Filling evenly into centers of cups. Return to oven and bake until filling is warm (about 4 minutes). Remove from baking sheets and let cool briefly on racks, then serve warm; or cool completely and serve at room temperature. Makes 3 dozen appetizers.

Goat Cheese Filling. In a blender or food processor, combine ½ cup (about 5 oz.) crumbled, firmly packed **ripened chèvre** (goat cheese) such as Bûcheron; 2 teaspoons **dry white wine;** ½ teaspoon **rubbed sage;** and 1 small clove **garlic,** chopped. Whirl until smoothly blended. If made ahead, cover and refrigerate for up to 1 week. Bring to room temperature before using.

SAUSAGE-CHEESE SQUARES

Custardy sausage squares can be served hot as an entrée, cooled as an appetizer. (To serve as a main course, cut into about nine large rectangles.)

> 2 **pounds mild or hot Italian sausages**
> 1 **large onion, finely chopped**
> 2 **cloves garlic, pressed or minced**
> ¼ **pound mushrooms, sliced**
> ½ **teaspoon** *each* **dry basil, dry mint, and oregano leaves**
> ¼ **cup chopped parsley**
> 8 **eggs**
> ⅓ **cup fine dry bread crumbs**
> ¼ **cup grated Parmesan cheese**
> 4 **cups (1 lb.) shredded mozzarella cheese**

Remove casings from sausages and crumble meat into a wide frying pan. Cook over medium-high heat, stirring, until browned. Drain off and discard all but 2 tablespoons fat. Add onion, garlic, mushrooms, basil, mint, oregano, and parsley to sausage in pan; cook, stirring, until onion is soft.

In a large bowl, beat eggs until blended. Stir in bread crumbs, Parmesan cheese, mozzarella cheese, and sausage mixture; pour into a lightly greased 10- by 15-inch rimmed baking pan and spread out evenly. Bake in a 325° oven until mixture feels firm in center when lightly touched (30 to 35 minutes). Let cool. Cut into 1-inch squares. Makes 12½ dozen appetizers.

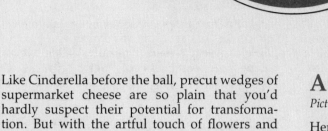

Like Cinderella before the ball, precut wedges of supermarket cheese are so plain that you'd hardly suspect their potential for transformation. But with the artful touch of flowers and herbs sealed beneath shimmering, transparent aspic, such a cheese can—like Cinderella—be the prettiest sight of the party.

Though decorated cheeses look like a caterer's specialty, they aren't difficult to prepare. If you can make gelatin, you won't have any trouble creating these glamorous additions to the appetizer tray. Once you've chosen the cheeses and selected greenery and flowers for garnish, spend a few minutes experimenting—decide on the most attractive arrangement of decorations before you make the glaze that will seal the pattern in place.

After glazing is completed, you can hold the cheeses in the refrigerator for up to 36 hours.

Choosing the cheeses. Any flat-surfaced cheese with an edible rind can be used, from your favorite jack or Cheddar to a full round of ripe Brie or Camembert. If you're combining several cheeses on a board or tray, select different shapes and sizes—one round, another rectangular, a third wedge-shaped or triangular. You'll also want cheeses with contrasting textures, such as a firm, a semisoft, and a soft.

Refrigerate cheeses until well chilled before glazing them. A cold surface helps the glaze adhere and set more quickly.

Edible decorations. Choose pesticide-free, well-washed herb leaves or sprigs and flower petals or entire small blossoms. Suggested greenery includes chives, dill, sage, thyme, tarragon, rosemary, watercress, cilantro, and parsley. Among the flowers (or petals) you might choose are pansies, roses, primroses, geraniums, carnations, nasturtiums, violets, and strawberry blossoms.

After rinsing leaves and flowers and blotting them dry with paper towels, store them in plastic bags in the refrigerator until you're ready to garnish the cheese.

ASPIC-GLAZED CHEESE

Pictured on facing page

Here's everything you need to decorate and glaze several cheeses. Wine will give a clearer, more sparkling aspic than broth.

> 2 **cups dry white wine or regular-strength chicken broth**
> 1 **envelope unflavored gelatin**
> **Flat-surfaced cheese (any rind must be edible), chilled**
> **Decorations (suggestions at left)**

In a 2- to 3-quart pan, combine wine and gelatin; let stand for 5 minutes. Place over medium heat and stir until gelatin is completely dissolved and mixture is clear.

Place pan in a larger container filled with ice water. Stir liquid occasionally (stir slowly so bubbles don't form) until it begins to thicken and look syrupy. If aspic becomes too firm, reheat to soften, then chill again until syrupy.

Set cold cheese on a rack in a shallow rimmed pan. Spoon a coat of aspic over top and sides of cheese; when aspic is slightly tacky (1 to 3 minutes), arrange decorations atop cheese in desired pattern. Refrigerate entire pan with rack and cheese, uncovered, for about 15 minutes.

Carefully spoon more aspic over top and sides of cheese; refrigerate until tacky. If necessary, add 1 or 2 more coats, refrigerating after each layer is added, in order to cover all exposed portions of decoration.

When cheese is completely covered with glaze, invert a bowl over cheese without touching surface and refrigerate until firm or for up to 36 hours.

Unused aspic (including drippings that collect in pan under rack) can be refrigerated, covered, for several days. Reheat to melt, then chill as before over a larger container of ice water until syrupy enough to coat cheese. Makes enough to coat six 3- by 5-inch rectangles of cheese with 3 layers of aspic.

Beneath a shimmering topcoat of aspic, flowers, herbs, and other greenery
dress up familiar cheeses—jack, the processed cheese called Gourmandise, Cheddar,
and Camembert. Instructions for Aspic-glazed Cheese are on the facing page.

VEGETABLE-CHEESE NACHOS

Crisp raw vegetables take the place of the usual tortilla chips in this quick-to-fix version of a popular appetizer.

    4 **cups assorted crisp raw vegetables (suggestions follow)**
    2 **cups (8 oz.) shredded jack or Cheddar cheese**
    2 **to 3 tablespoons** *each* **canned diced green chiles and sliced ripe olives**

Arrange vegetable pieces on a heatproof platter. Sprinkle evenly with cheese, chiles, and olives. Broil 4 to 6 inches below heat until cheese is melted (5 to 7 minutes). Makes 6 servings.

Assorted vegetables. Choose 2 or more from the following: **carrot** or **celery** sticks; **zucchini** or **crookneck squash** slices; **green** or **red bell pepper** strips; **jicama** or **turnip** sticks. Cut vegetables thick enough to scoop up cheese.

SALSA POTATO SKINS

Pictured on page 35

The skin is arguably the best part of a baked potato, even without a gilding coat of melted Cheddar and jack. With that coat, there is little question of it. Add a chile salsa dip and there's no question at all.

    5 **large russet potatoes (about 3 lbs.** *total*)
      Chile Salsa (recipe follows)
      About ⅓ cup butter or margarine, melted
  ¾ **cup** *each* **shredded mild Cheddar cheese and shredded jack cheese**

Scrub potatoes and pierce each in several places with a fork. Bake in a 400° oven until potatoes feel soft when squeezed (about 1 hour). Meanwhile, prepare Chile Salsa and set aside.

Let potatoes stand until cool enough to handle. Cut each potato lengthwise into quarters. With a spoon, scoop flesh from skins, leaving a ⅛-inch-thick shell. Reserve flesh for other uses.

Brush potato skins inside and out with butter. Place, skin side down, in a single layer on a 12- by 15-inch baking sheet. Bake in a 500° oven until crisp (about 12 minutes). Remove from oven and distrib-

ute Cheddar and jack cheeses among hot skins, filling equally.

Broil 4 inches below heat until cheeses are melted (about 2 minutes). Serve with Chile Salsa for dipping. Makes 20 appetizers.

Chile Salsa. Stir together 1 can (8 oz.) **tomato sauce**, 1 can (4 oz.) **diced green chiles**, and ¼ cup chopped **green onions** (including tops). Pour salsa into a small serving bowl.

If made ahead, cover and refrigerate for up to 24 hours.

CHEESE & BACON IN A BREAD BOAT

A smooth, rich mixture of cream cheese, bacon bits, and green onions fills a hollowed French loaf. Chunks of bread, toasted crisp and golden, make crunchy scoops for the creamy filling.

    1 **pound bacon, diced**
    1 **round or oval loaf (1½ lbs.) French bread**
    1 **large package (8 oz.) cream cheese, softened**
    1 **cup sour cream**
  ½ **cup chopped green bell pepper**
  ½ **cup thinly sliced green onions (including tops)**

In a wide frying pan, cook bacon over medium heat, stirring constantly, until crisp. Lift out bacon with a slotted spoon; set aside. Reserve 3 tablespoons drippings.

Using a serrated knife and your fingers, remove center of bread in a single piece, leaving a shell about ½ inch thick on sides and bottom. Cut removed bread into 1½- by 2-inch chunks about ½ inch thick.

Brush inside of bread shell with reserved 3 tablespoons bacon drippings. Place shell and bread chunks in a single layer on two 10- by 15-inch baking sheets. Bake in a 350° oven for about 15 minutes.

Meanwhile, in a bowl, beat together cream cheese and sour cream; stir in bell pepper, onions, and bacon. Remove bread from oven. Place bread chunks on racks; pour cheese mixture into shell. Return shell to oven and bake until cheese mixture is hot (15 to 20 minutes). Place filled shell on a serving board and surround with toasted bread chunks. To eat, dip bread chunks into cheese; once chunks have been eaten, break up bread shell to use for dipping. Makes 10 to 12 servings.

MINI-QUICHES

Pictured on page 32

These two-bite appetizers can be made a day ahead, then reheated.

    Flaky Pastry (recipe follows)
    Bacon & Mushroom Filling or Ham &
    Green Chile Filling (recipes follow)
2 **eggs**
¾ **cup sour cream**

Prepare Flaky Pastry. Prepare your choice of filling and set aside.

On a lightly floured board, roll out pastry ¹⁄₁₆ inch thick. Cut into 2-inch circles. Reroll scraps and cut again to make a total of 72 circles. Fit each circle into a 1¾-inch muffin cup; pastry should cover bottom of cup and come partway up sides.

Place a heaping teaspoon of filling in each cup. In a bowl, lightly beat eggs; add sour cream and beat until smooth. Spoon about 1 teaspoon of the egg mixture over filling in each cup. Bake in a 375° oven until filling is puffed and lightly browned on top (20 to 25 minutes). Let quiches cool in pans on racks for 5 minutes; remove from pans and serve warm. Or let cool completely and serve at room temperature.

If made ahead, wrap cooled quiches airtight and refrigerate for up to 24 hours. To reheat, unwrap quiches and arrange on a baking sheet. Bake in a 350° oven for about 10 minutes. Makes 6 dozen appetizers.

Flaky Pastry. In a bowl, stir together 2 cups **all-purpose flour** and ½ teaspoon **salt**. Add ½ teaspoon **caraway seeds** if using Bacon & Mushroom Filling; add ½ teaspoon **chili powder** if using Ham & Green Chile Filling.

Using a pastry blender or 2 knives, cut in ⅓ cup firm **butter** or margarine until fat particles are the size of peas. Add ⅓ cup chilled **solid vegetable shortening;** cut in until mixture resembles fine crumbs. In a glass measure, beat 1 **egg;** add enough **cold water** to make ¼ cup. Add egg-water mixture to flour mixture, 1 tablespoon at a time, mixing with a fork until dough holds together. Gather dough into a ball with your hands. Wrap in plastic wrap and refrigerate for 1 hour.

Bacon & Mushroom Filling. In a wide frying pan, cook 6 slices **bacon** over medium heat until crisp; drain, crumble, and set aside. Discard bacon drippings. Melt 1 tablespoon **butter** or margarine in pan; add ¼ pound **mushrooms,** chopped. Cook, stirring often, until liquid has evaporated. Remove from heat. Stir in bacon, ¼ cup chopped **green onions** (including tops), and 1½ cups (6 oz.) shredded **Swiss cheese.**

Ham & Green Chile Filling. In a bowl, mix ¾ cup finely diced **cooked ham,** 3 tablespoons **canned diced green chiles,** ¼ cup chopped **green onions** (including tops), and 1½ cups (6 oz.) shredded **jack cheese.**

APPETIZER CHEESE PUFFS

These golden puff-pastry bites look a bit like ravioli and are shaped in much the same way. Each little puff is filled with sharp Cheddar and green chiles and topped with a sprinkling of sesame seeds.

    Cheese & Chile Filling (recipe follows)
1 **package (17¼ oz.) frozen puff pastry, thawed**
1 **egg, beaten**
2 **tablespoons sesame seeds**

Prepare filling and set aside.

Carefully unfold thawed puff-pastry sheets. On a floured board, roll each pastry sheet out to a 12- by 15-inch rectangle. Drop rounded teaspoons of filling on half of each sheet (a 6- by 15-inch area); make 3 rows of 5 dollops each, spacing them about ¾ inch apart and ½ inch from edges and center of pastry.

Brush egg around edges of pastry and between dollops of filling. Fold unfilled side of pastry over so edges meet. With a fork, prick pastry several times over each filling mound; then press pastry firmly around each mound to seal well. With a ravioli cutter or a sharp knife, cut between mounds. Arrange puffs, slightly apart, on 2 ungreased 10- by 15-inch baking sheets. Cover with plastic wrap and refrigerate until cold (at least 30 minutes) or for up to 8 hours. Also cover and refrigerate remaining egg.

Cut a ½-inch-long slash in top of each puff. Brush puffs with remaining egg and sprinkle with sesame seeds. Bake in a 400° oven until golden (15 to 20 minutes). Serve hot or warm. Makes 2½ dozen appetizers.

Cheese & Chile Filling. In a medium-size bowl, beat together 2 small packages (3 oz. *each*) **cream cheese,** softened; 1¾ cups (7 oz.) shredded **sharp Cheddar cheese;** and ⅓ cup well-drained **canned diced green chiles.**

The soul-warming riches of French Onion Soup (facing page) begin with slow-cooked onions and end with a crown of crusty bread topped by Parmesan and sweet, nutty Swiss cheeses.

SOUPS

Soups and the melting cheeses are traditional companions in many cuisines, but—surprise—bloomy-rind and fresh cheeses are possibilities, as well.

◆ COLD TOMATO SOUP WITH SHRIMP ◆

Chunks of mild cream cheese tone down the zesty flavor of this cold soup. Try it as a lunch entrée, accompanied with buttered bagels and fresh fruit.

- 4 cups clam-flavored tomato cocktail or tomato juice
- ½ cup chopped peeled cucumber
- ⅓ cup thinly sliced green onions (including tops)
- ¼ pound small cooked shrimp
- 2 tablespoons red wine vinegar
- 2 tablespoons olive oil or salad oil
- 1 tablespoon sugar
- 1 teaspoon dill weed
- 1 clove garlic, minced or pressed
- 1 small package (3 oz.) cream cheese, cut into ¼-inch cubes
- ¼ to ½ teaspoon liquid hot pepper seasoning
- 1 medium-size avocado

In a large bowl, combine tomato cocktail, cucumber, onions, shrimp, vinegar, oil, sugar, dill weed, garlic, and cream cheese. Stir well; then stir in hot pepper seasoning. Cover and refrigerate until well chilled (about 30 minutes) or until next day. Pit, peel, and dice avocado just before serving; stir into soup. Makes 4 servings.

◆ FRENCH ONION SOUP ◆

Pictured on facing page

Slow-cooked caramelized onions and a touch of port wine give this classic soup its mellow sweetness. Each bowlful wears a crunchy, golden crown of crisp toast topped with Swiss and Parmesan cheeses.

- 4 tablespoons butter or margarine
- 1 tablespoon olive oil or salad oil
- 6 large onions, thinly sliced
  Dry-toasted French Bread (page 48)
- 6 cups regular-strength beef broth
  Salt and pepper
- ⅓ cup port
- ½ cup diced Swiss cheese
- ½ cup shredded Swiss cheese
- ½ cup grated Parmesan cheese

Melt 2 tablespoons of the butter in oil in a 4- to 5-quart pan over medium-low heat. Add onions and cook, stirring occasionally, until very soft and caramel-colored but not browned (about 40 minutes). Meanwhile, prepare Dry-toasted French Bread and set aside. Add broth to onions and bring to a boil over high heat; then reduce heat, cover, and simmer for 30 minutes. Season to taste with salt and pepper; stir in port.

Pour soup into six 1½- to 2-cup ovenproof soup bowls. Evenly top each serving with diced Swiss cheese, then with a piece of toast, buttered side up. Sprinkle evenly with shredded Swiss cheese, then with Parmesan cheese. Melt remaining 2 tablespoons butter in a small pan; drizzle evenly over cheese-topped toast.

Place bowls on a rimmed baking sheet. Bake in a 425° oven for 10 minutes; then broil about 4 inches below heat until cheese is lightly browned (about 2 minutes). Serve immediately. Makes 6 servings.

◆ GOLDEN YAM SOUP ◆

Golden vegetables and Cheddar blend intriguingly in a smooth first-course soup. Use leftover cooked yams if you have them on hand. Or bake fresh ones in a 400° oven until soft when squeezed (about 50 minutes); then cool, peel, and mash.

- 3 tablespoons butter or margarine
- 1 medium-size onion, chopped
- 2 medium-size carrots, cut into ¼-inch-thick slices
- 1 green bell pepper, seeded and chopped
- 2 cups regular-strength chicken broth
- ½ teaspoon ground cinnamon
- 2 cups mashed cooked yams
- 2 cups milk
- 1 cup (4 oz.) shredded sharp Cheddar cheese
- 2 tablespoons Worcestershire
  Salt and pepper

(Continued on next page)

Melt butter in a 4-quart pan over medium heat. Add onion, carrots, and bell pepper; cook, stirring occasionally, until onion is soft. Stir in broth and cinnamon.

Bring to a boil over high heat; reduce heat, cover, and simmer until carrots are very tender when pierced (15 to 20 minutes).

Stir yams into broth mixture. Then whirl mixture, a portion at a time, in a blender until smooth. Return to pan, stir in milk, and heat until steaming. Add cheese, about ⅓ cup at a time, stirring until melted after each addition. Stir in Worcestershire; season to taste with salt and pepper. Makes about 8 servings.

LEEK SOUP WITH BRIE

In this cousin of French Onion Soup (page 47), flavorful Brie melts atop slices of toast, taking the place of the usual Swiss cheese.

Dry-toasted French Bread (recipe follows)
6 large leeks (about 3 lbs. *total*)
2 tablespoons butter or margarine
½ pound mushrooms, thinly sliced
1 clove garlic, minced or pressed
½ teaspoon dry tarragon
¼ teaspoon white pepper
2½ tablespoons all-purpose flour
4 cups regular-strength chicken broth
⅓ cup whipping cream
8 ounces Brie cheese

Prepare Dry-toasted French Bread. Set aside.

Trim and discard ends and tops of leeks, leaving about 3 inches of dark green leaves. Discard tough outer leaves. Split leeks lengthwise; rinse well, then thinly slice crosswise.

Melt butter in a 4- to 5-quart pan over medium heat. Add leeks, mushrooms, garlic, tarragon, and white pepper. Cook, stirring, until vegetables are very soft and almost all liquid has evaporated (about 15 minutes). Stir in flour; cook, stirring, until bubbly. Stir in broth and cream; bring to a boil over medium-high heat, stirring constantly.

Pour soup into six 1½- to 2-cup ovenproof soup bowls. Top each serving with a piece of toast, buttered side up. Cut cheese into ½-inch-thick slices, then arrange cheese on toast to cover. Place bowls on a rimmed baking sheet. Bake in a 425° oven for 10 minutes; then broil about 6 inches below heat until cheese is lightly browned (1 to 2 minutes). Serve immediately. Makes 6 servings.

Dry-toasted French Bread. Cut 6 slices **French bread,** each ½ inch thick, to fit inside six 1½- to 2-cup ovenproof soup bowls. Place bread on a baking sheet and bake in a 325° oven until lightly toasted (20 to 25 minutes). Spread one side of each slice with 1 teaspoon **butter** or margarine.

CREAMY LEEK & EDAM SOUP

The gentle flavor of Edam cheese tempers the sharper nip of leeks in a country-style milk soup from Holland.

4 medium-size leeks (1 to 1½ lbs. *total*)
¾ cup all-purpose flour
8 cups regular-strength beef broth
1 cup milk
⅛ teaspoon *each* pepper and ground mace
¼ cup whipping cream
4 cups (1 lb.) shredded Edam cheese

Trim and discard ends and tops of leeks, leaving about 3 inches of dark green leaves. Discard tough outer leaves. Split leeks lengthwise; rinse well, then thinly slice crosswise. Set aside.

Place flour in a 5- to 6-quart pan. Smoothly blend in broth, a little at a time. Stir in milk, pepper, and mace. Place over medium-high heat and bring to a boil, stirring constantly; reduce heat, cover, and simmer for 10 minutes, stirring occasionally. Stir in leeks and cream; cover and simmer, stirring occasionally, until leeks are tender to bite (about 10 more minutes).

Pass cheese at the table to sprinkle over individual servings. Makes about 8 servings.

CORN CHOWDER WITH CHEESE

Cheddar and chowder are two of the grand old institutions of New England cuisine. Here they come together in one hearty soup.

3 tablespoons butter or margarine
1 clove garlic, minced or pressed
2 large onions, chopped
4 cups regular-strength chicken broth
½ teaspoon thyme leaves
1 bay leaf
1 pound thin-skinned potatoes
1 package (1 lb.) frozen whole-kernel corn, thawed
2 cups milk
½ cup whipping cream
   Salt and pepper
1½ cups (6 oz.) shredded sharp Cheddar cheese

Melt butter in a 5- to 6-quart pan over medium heat. Add garlic and onions; cook, stirring, until onions are soft. Stir in broth, thyme, and bay leaf; bring to a boil.

Meanwhile, cut potatoes into ½-inch cubes. Add to boiling broth; reduce heat, cover, and simmer until potatoes are tender when pierced (10 to 15 minutes).

Stir in corn, milk, and cream. Stir soup over low heat until steaming; do not let soup boil. Season to taste with salt and pepper. Pass cheese at the table to sprinkle over individual servings. Makes 4 to 6 servings.

◆ BEER CHEER CHEESE SOUP ◆

Beer, cheese, and pretzels get along as usual, even in an unusual soup. Teamed with a salad or sandwich, a bowl of the soup makes a satisfying light meal.

¼ cup butter or margarine
½ cup *each* thinly sliced celery, diced carrot, and chopped onion
½ cup all-purpose flour
½ teaspoon dry mustard
¼ teaspoon thyme leaves
4 cups regular-strength chicken broth
1½ cups (6 oz.) shredded sharp Cheddar cheese
2 tablespoons grated Parmesan cheese
1 can (12 oz.) beer
   Salt and pepper
   Pretzels

Melt butter in a 3-quart pan over medium heat. Add celery, carrot, and onion; cook, stirring occasionally, until onion is soft.

Stir in flour, mustard, and thyme and cook, stirring, for 1 minute. Gradually stir in broth. Increase heat to medium-high and bring to a boil, stirring often. Reduce heat, cover, and simmer, stirring often, until carrots are very tender to bite (12 to 15 minutes).

Add Cheddar cheese, a handful at a time, stirring until melted after each addition. Stir in Parmesan cheese, then gradually stir in beer. Heat until steaming, stirring often. Season to taste with salt and pepper. Serve with pretzels. Makes 4 to 6 servings.

◆ CURRIED BROCCOLI & CHEDDAR SOUP ◆

Winter vegetables—broccoli, onions, potatoes, and carrots—are the backbone of this spicy soup. It's an excellent choice for a cold-weather lunch or light supper. Shredded Cheddar, added just before serving, harmonizes the flavors and textures of the diverse ingredients.

   About 1½ pounds broccoli
¼ cup butter or margarine
1 tablespoon curry powder
1 medium-size onion, chopped
6 cups regular-strength chicken broth
2 large thin-skinned potatoes, cubed
4 slender carrots, thinly sliced
1 cup milk
3 cups (12 oz.) shredded sharp Cheddar cheese

Trim flowerets from broccoli and cut into small pieces. Cut off and discard tough stalk ends; peel stalks and slice thinly. Set aside.

Melt butter in a 6- to 8-quart pan over medium heat; add curry powder and onion. Cook, stirring, for 5 minutes. Stir in broth, broccoli stalks, potatoes, and carrots; reduce heat, cover, and simmer until potatoes mash very easily (about 30 minutes). Whirl about half the broth and vegetables at a time in a blender or food processor until smoothly puréed. Return purée to pan.

Bring soup to a boil; stir in broccoli flowerets and milk. Reduce heat and simmer, uncovered, just until flowerets are tender when pierced. Add cheese, a handful at a time, stirring until melted after each addition. Serve immediately. Makes 8 to 10 servings.

SANDWICHES & PIZZA

Good old melted Cheddar on toast has scores of inviting cousins from around the world. Pizza is just as open to variations on its main theme.

◆ TOSTAS ◆

These grilled cheese sandwiches make imaginative use of cheeses and condiments. They often show up at informal suppers or impromptu parties.

> 4 to 8 ounces fontina or tybo cheese, sliced
> 8 to 12 ounces jack cheese, sliced
> ½ to ¾ pound sliced cooked ham
> ¼ to ½ pound thinly sliced prosciutto (optional)
> 1 loaf (1 lb.) sliced egg bread, Italian bread, or French bread
> Condiments (suggestions follow)

Have all ingredients assembled and close at hand. To make each tosta, place 1 or 2 slices of each cheese and 1 or 2 slices of ham and/or prosciutto between 2 slices of bread. Toast sandwiches in an ungreased sandwich grill on medium-high heat or in an ungreased wide frying pan, covered, over medium heat. Cook, turning as needed, until sandwiches are browned on both sides and cheese is melted. Let diners open sandwiches and add their choice of condiments. Be sure to provide plenty of napkins; sandwiches are messy to eat. Makes about 6 servings.

Russian Dressing. In a small bowl, blend ⅔ cup **mayonnaise** with ¼ cup drained **sweet pickle relish** and 2 tablespoons **tomato-based chili sauce.** Cover and refrigerate until serving time.

Artichokes. Use 2 jars (6 oz. *each*) **marinated artichoke hearts,** drained and cut into thin slices.

Red pepper. Seed and sliver 1 large **red bell pepper.** Heat 2 tablespoons **olive oil** in a small frying pan over medium-high heat. Add bell pepper and 2 tablespoons **water** and cook, covered, until liquid evaporates. Remove cover and stir in 1 tablespoon **red wine vinegar** and season to taste with **salt.** Serve at room temperature. (Or use one 8-ounce jar roasted red peppers.)

Onion. Cut 1 large **mild white onion** in half lengthwise; cut each half lengthwise into thin slivers. Combine onion, ¼ cup **water,** and 2 tablespoons **white wine vinegar** in a wide frying pan. Bring to a boil over medium-high heat; boil, stirring, until liquid has evaporated and onion is soft. Remove from heat and season to taste with **salt.** Let cool to room temperature before serving. (Or use one 6-ounce jar pickled onions, drained and thinly sliced.)

Mushrooms. Thinly slice ½ pound **mushrooms.** Heat 2 tablespoons **olive oil** in a medium-size frying pan over medium heat. Add mushrooms and cook, stirring, until soft; add 2 tablespoons **white wine vinegar** and cook until liquid has evaporated. (Or use one 5-ounce jar marinated mushrooms, drained and thinly sliced.)

Caponata. Use 1 can (5 oz.) **eggplant caponata** or use homemade caponata.

Pickled peppers. Use 1 jar (about 8 oz.) **Italian-style pickled peppers** (peperoncini).

◆ TOASTED JACK CHEESE & MUSHROOM SANDWICHES ◆

Hot from the broiler, this open-faced sandwich makes a satisfying quick lunch or supper when served with hot soup.

> 3 tablespoons butter or margarine
> ½ pound mushrooms, sliced
> 4 slices light rye bread
> 2 medium-size tomatoes, peeled and sliced
> 6 ounces jack cheese, sliced
> Parsley sprigs

Melt 2 tablespoons of the butter in a wide frying pan over medium heat. Add mushrooms and cook, stirring, until liquid has evaporated. Remove from heat. Toast bread. Spread remaining 1 tablespoon butter evenly over toast; place toast on a baking sheet. Reserve ⅓ of the mushrooms for topping. Evenly spoon remaining mushrooms over toast; arrange an even layer of tomatoes over mushrooms. Cover tomatoes evenly with cheese.

Broil about 4 inches below heat until cheese is melted. Spoon reserved mushrooms over sandwiches; then garnish with parsley sprigs. Makes 4 sandwiches.

In Sausage, Olive & Artichoke Pizza (page 52), as in other versions of
this perennial favorite, it's the mild-flavored, stringy mozzarella that holds
the various toppings together. Try a refreshing spinach salad alongside.

Monte Cristo Sandwich

The Monte Cristo is one of the more elegant of toasted ham and cheese sandwiches. Omit the turkey and it becomes a Monte Carlo.

12 slices firm-textured white bread
    Mayonnaise
12 slices Swiss cheese, *each* about ⅛ inch thick
 6 slices cooked ham, *each* ⅛ to ¼ inch thick
 6 slices cooked turkey, *each* ⅛ to ¼ inch thick
 3 eggs
 ¼ cup half-and-half, light cream, or milk
    Dash of salt
 3 to 5 tablespoons butter or margarine
    Powdered sugar
    Parsley sprigs
    Red currant jelly

Thinly spread one side of each bread slice with mayonnaise. Then assemble 6 sandwiches, using 2 slices of cheese, one slice of ham, and one slice of turkey for each sandwich. Trim bread crusts and filling with a sharp knife, making edges of sandwiches even; cut each sandwich in half diagonally.

In a shallow dish, beat eggs, half-and-half, and salt until blended. Place sandwiches in mixture and turn to coat; then let stand, turning occasionally, until all liquid is absorbed. Melt about 3 tablespoons of the butter in a wide frying pan over medium heat. Add as many sandwiches as will fit without crowding; cook, turning once, until lightly browned on both sides. Remove from pan. Repeat with remaining sandwiches, adding more butter to pan as needed.

Place the sandwiches on an ungreased baking sheet and bake in a 400° oven until cheese is melted (3 to 5 minutes). Dust with powdered sugar and garnish with parsley sprigs. Serve hot, accompanied with jelly. Makes 6 sandwiches.

Blintz Toast Sandwiches

Delight brunch guests with this unexpected combination of the Eastern European blintz and French toast.

1½ cups small curd cottage cheese
 1 teaspoon grated lemon peel
 2 tablespoons granulated sugar
12 slices stale or dry firm-textured white bread, crusts removed
 3 eggs
 ⅓ cup milk
 3 to 5 tablespoons butter or margarine
    Powdered sugar
    Cherry preserves or jam

In a bowl, stir together cottage cheese, lemon peel, and granulated sugar. Spread the cheese mixture evenly over 6 of the bread slices, then top each with another slice.

In a shallow dish, beat eggs and milk until blended. Place sandwiches in mixture and turn to coat; then let stand, turning occasionally, until all liquid is absorbed.

Melt about 3 tablespoons of the butter in a wide frying pan over medium heat. Add as many sandwiches as will fit without crowding; cook, turning carefully, until golden on both sides. Remove from pan and keep warm. Repeat with remaining sandwiches, adding more butter to pan as needed.

Arrange sandwiches on plates and sprinkle with powdered sugar; top with preserves. Makes 6 sandwiches.

Sausage, Olive & Artichoke Pizza

Pictured on page 51

Marinated artichoke hearts, sliced ripe olives, a rich tomato sauce liberally seasoned with spicy Italian sausage, and plenty of shredded mozzarella cheese make this pizza a traditional favorite.

 1 package active dry yeast
 ½ teaspoon sugar
 ½ cup warm water (110°F)
 ¼ teaspoon salt
1½ tablespoons olive oil or salad oil
1⅓ cups all-purpose flour
    Sausage-Tomato Sauce (recipe follows)
    Cornmeal
    Olive oil or salad oil
 2 tablespoons grated Parmesan cheese
 1 jar (6 oz.) marinated artichoke hearts, drained
 1 can (2¼ oz.) sliced ripe olives, drained
1½ cups (6 oz.) shredded mozzarella cheese

In a large bowl, dissolve yeast and sugar in warm water. Let stand for 5 minutes. Stir in salt, the 1½ tablespoons oil, and 1 cup of the flour; beat with a heavy spoon until dough is elastic and pulls away from bowl sides. Scrape dough out onto a board sprinkled with remaining ⅓ cup flour. Knead until dough is smooth and elastic, with small bubbles just beneath the surface (5 to 10 minutes). Place dough in a greased bowl and turn over to grease top; cover and let rise in a warm place until doubled (45 to 60 minutes).

Meanwhile, prepare sauce. Grease an 11-inch pizza pan or a 12- by 15-inch baking sheet, then dust with cornmeal and set aside.

Punch down dough, turn out onto a floured board, and knead briefly to release air; then roll out to an 11-inch circle. Lift dough onto prepared pan; brush lightly with oil. Spread sauce evenly over dough to within ½ inch of edges. Sprinkle with Parmesan cheese, then top with artichokes and olives. Sprinkle with mozzarella cheese.

Bake on lowest rack of a 450° oven until crust is well browned (15 to 20 minutes). Let stand for 5 minutes; cut into wedges. Makes one 11-inch pizza.

Sausage-Tomato Sauce. Remove casings from ½ pound **mild Italian sausages** and crumble meat into a wide frying pan. Add 1 tablespoon **olive oil** and cook over medium-high heat, stirring frequently, until meat is no longer pink. Add 1 **onion,** chopped, and 1 clove **garlic,** minced or pressed. Continue to cook, stirring, until onion is soft. Add 1 can (about 15 oz.) **pear-shaped tomatoes** (break up with a spoon) and their liquid; ½ teaspoon **dry basil;** ¼ teaspoon **oregano leaves;** and ¼ cup **dry white wine.** Cook, stirring frequently, until almost all liquid has evaporated (about 10 minutes).

 # CALZONE

Folding pizza on itself makes the plump turnover called *calzone*. These crusty turnovers contain a spicy sausage or hearty vegetable filling rich with melting mozzarella and Parmesan.

- 1 **package active dry yeast**
- 1 **cup warm water (110°F)**
- ½ **teaspoon salt**
- 2 **teaspoons olive oil or salad oil**
- 2¾ **to 3 cups all-purpose flour**
  Sausage Filling or Vegetable Filling (recipes follow)
  Cornmeal
  Olive oil or salad oil

In a large bowl, dissolve yeast in warm water. Let stand for 5 minutes. Stir in salt and the 2 teaspoons oil. With a heavy spoon, gradually beat in about 2½ cups of the flour or enough to make a dough that is soft but not too sticky to knead.

Turn dough out onto a well-floured board and knead until smooth and elastic, adding more flour as needed to prevent sticking. Place dough in a greased bowl and turn over to grease top. Cover and let rise in a warm place until doubled (about 1 hour).

Meanwhile, prepare filling of your choice. Grease two 10- by 15-inch baking sheets; dust lightly with cornmeal and set aside.

Punch down dough, turn out onto a lightly floured board, and knead briefly to release air. Then divide dough in half for 2 large turnovers, in quarters for 4 individual turnovers. Shape each portion into a ball; roll large balls out to 11-inch circles, small balls to 8½-inch circles. Brush surface of each circle lightly with oil.

Spread filling evenly over half of each circle to within about ½ inch of edge. (Use half the filling for each large circle, ¼ of the filling for each small circle.) Fold other half of each circle over filling; press edges together. Roll ½ inch of pressed edges up and over; seal and crimp. With a wide spatula, transfer turnovers to prepared baking sheets. Prick tops with a fork, then brush lightly with oil. Bake in a 475° oven until well browned (15 to 20 minutes for either size). Serve hot. Makes 4 servings.

Sausage Filling. Slice 10 ounces **mild Italian sausages.** Cook sliced sausages in a wide frying pan over medium heat until browned. Spoon off and discard all but 2 tablespoons fat. Add 1 small **onion,** thinly sliced; 1 clove **garlic,** minced or pressed; ¼ pound **mushrooms,** sliced; 1 small **green bell pepper,** seeded and cut into thin strips; and 1 small **carrot,** thinly sliced. Cook, stirring, until vegetables are soft. Stir in 1 can (8 oz.) **tomato sauce,** 1 can (2¼ oz.) **sliced ripe olives** (drained), 1 teaspoon **dry basil,** ½ teaspoon *each* **oregano leaves** and **sugar,** and ¼ teaspoon **crushed red pepper.**

Reduce heat and simmer, uncovered, for about 5 minutes. Remove from heat and let cool. When ready to assemble calzone, stir in 2 cups (8 oz.) shredded **mozzarella cheese** and ½ cup grated **Parmesan cheese.** Season to taste with **salt** and **pepper.**

Vegetable Filling. Follow directions for **Sausage Filling,** but omit sausages. Cook vegetables in 2 to 3 tablespoons **olive oil** or salad oil; increase mushrooms to ½ pound. Also increase oregano leaves to 1 teaspoon; add ½ teaspoon **fennel seeds,** if desired. Increase mozzarella cheese to 2½ cups, Parmesan cheese to ¾ cup.

The fragile soufflé has a short life, so have your dining audience assembled
at the table before you present this high and handsome entrée. Spinach & Cheese Soufflé
(facing page) is perfect for a festive brunch or for an informal lunch or supper.

SOUFFLÉS & OMELETS

Both soufflés and omelets are satisfying ways to use up the last bits of almost any cheese in the world. These soufflés demonstrate deliciously that even as dense a cheese as Cheddar can be transformed into something light and airy. You can vary the flavor from subtle Swiss to more assertive goat or blue-veined cheeses, or even to bold Limburger. Heartier omelets and frittatas usually pair cheese with vegetables, herbs, and other ingredients.

◆ CHEESE SOUFFLÉ ◆

A light and delicate soufflé enhances any special occasion. To vary this classic, sprinkle the buttered dish with freshly grated Parmesan cheese before adding the egg mixture. Or you can substitute one of the Swiss cheeses or almost any other firm cheese for the Cheddar in this recipe.

3½ tablespoons butter or margarine
3 tablespoons all-purpose flour
   Dash of ground red pepper (cayenne)
¼ teaspoon *each* dry mustard and salt
1 cup milk
1 cup (4 oz.) shredded sharp Cheddar cheese
4 eggs, separated

Preheat oven to 375°. Generously butter a 1½-quart soufflé dish, using ½ tablespoon of the butter.

Melt remaining 3 tablespoons butter in a 2-quart pan over medium heat. Add flour, red pepper, mustard, and salt; cook, stirring, until bubbly. Remove from heat and gradually stir in milk. Return to heat and cook, stirring constantly, until sauce boils and thickens. Add cheese and stir until melted. Remove from heat; thoroughly beat in egg yolks. Set aside.

In a large bowl, beat egg whites until they hold soft, moist peaks. Thoroughly fold about ⅓ of the beaten whites into cheese sauce to lighten it; then fold in remaining whites. Pour mixture into prepared soufflé dish. With the tip of a knife, draw a circle on surface of soufflé about 1 inch in from rim of dish. Bake until top of soufflé is golden brown and center feels firm when lightly tapped (about 35 minutes). Serve immediately. Makes 4 servings.

◆ SPINACH & CHEESE SOUFFLÉ ◆

Pictured on facing page

Just a small change can give an old favorite a new look. Here, the addition of chopped cooked spinach adds interest to a plain cheese soufflé.

3½ tablespoons butter or margarine
3 tablespoons all-purpose flour
½ teaspoon *each* dry tarragon and salt
⅛ teaspoon ground nutmeg
1 cup milk
1 cup (4 oz.) shredded Swiss cheese
6 eggs, separated
½ cup cooked, squeezed, chopped spinach

Preheat oven to 375°. Generously butter a 2-quart soufflé dish, using ½ tablespoon of the butter.

Melt remaining 3 tablespoons butter in a 3-quart pan over medium heat. Add flour, tarragon, salt, and nutmeg; cook, stirring, until bubbly. Remove from heat and gradually stir in milk. Return to heat and cook, stirring constantly, until sauce boils and thickens. Add cheese and stir until melted. Remove from heat; thoroughly beat in egg yolks. Stir in spinach. Set aside.

In a large bowl, beat egg whites until they hold soft, moist peaks. Thoroughly fold about ⅓ of the beaten whites into cheese sauce to lighten it; then fold in remaining whites.

Pour mixture into prepared soufflé dish. Bake until top of soufflé is golden brown and center feels firm when lightly tapped (30 to 35 minutes). Serve immediately. Makes 4 to 6 servings.

◆ BOLD CHEESE SOUFFLÉ ◆

Just as bold-flavored cheeses transform omelets and crêpes from predictable to exciting, so they make stunning surprises of soufflés. The flavors are distinctive, but milder than one might expect.

3½ tablespoons butter or margarine
   About 2 tablespoons grated Parmesan cheese
¼ cup all-purpose flour
1 cup milk
5 to 7 ounces bold cheese (suggestions on page 56), broken or cut into small pieces
6 eggs, separated

(Continued on next page)

Preheat oven to 375°. Generously butter a 2-quart baking dish, using ½ tablespoon of the butter. Dust buttered dish with Parmesan cheese.

Melt remaining 3 tablespoons butter in a 3-quart pan over medium heat. Add flour and cook, stirring, until bubbly. Remove from heat and gradually stir in milk. Return to heat and cook, stirring constantly, until sauce boils and thickens. Add bold cheese of your choice and stir until melted. Remove from heat; thoroughly beat in egg yolks. Set aside.

In a large bowl, beat egg whites until they hold soft, moist peaks. Thoroughly fold about ⅓ of the beaten whites into cheese sauce to lighten it; then fold in remaining whites.

Pour mixture into prepared soufflé dish. Bake until top of soufflé is golden brown and center feels firm when lightly tapped (30 to 35 minutes). Serve immediately. Makes 4 to 6 servings.

Bold cheeses. The following assertive cheeses work well in soufflés.

Soft-ripened cheeses such as Brie and Camembert, and their double- and triple-cream cousins (see pages 14 and 15).

Monastery and other washed-rind, semisoft cheeses, including Port du Salut, Münster, Beer Cheese, and even Limburger (see pages 26 to 28).

Blue-veined cheeses such as Gorgonzola, Roquefort, and Stilton, or the creamier versions such as Blue Castello (see pages 12 and 13).

Goat cheeses ranging from the mild, unripened Montrachet to riper Bûcheron (see page 21).

◆ CAMEMBERT SOUFFLÉ ◆

Blending bold Camembert with milder cheeses produces an extra-rich soufflé that's ideal for brunch.

4½ tablespoons butter or margarine
    About 2 tablespoons grated Parmesan cheese
  3 tablespoons all-purpose flour
  ¼ teaspoon ground nutmeg
  ⅛ teaspoon ground red pepper (cayenne)
1⅓ cups milk
  2 teaspoons Dijon mustard
  2 tablespoons dry sherry
  4 ounces ripe Camembert cheese (rind removed), cut into small pieces
1¼ cups (5 oz.) shredded Gruyère, Samsoe, or Swiss cheese
  5 eggs, separated
  ¼ teaspoon *each* cream of tartar and salt

Preheat oven to 375°. Generously butter a 2-quart soufflé dish, using ½ tablespoon of the butter. Dust buttered dish with Parmesan cheese.

Melt remaining 4 tablespoons butter in a 3-quart pan over medium heat. Add flour, nutmeg, and red pepper; cook, stirring, until bubbly. Remove from heat and gradually stir in milk. Return to heat and cook, stirring constantly, until sauce boils and thickens. Add mustard, sherry, Camembert cheese, and Gruyère cheese; stir until cheese is melted. Remove from heat; thoroughly beat in egg yolks. Return to heat and cook, stirring, for 1 minute; set aside.

In a large bowl, combine egg whites, cream of tartar, and salt. Beat until egg whites hold soft, moist peaks. Thoroughly fold about ⅓ of the beaten whites into cheese sauce to lighten it; then fold in remaining whites. Pour into prepared soufflé dish.

Bake until top of soufflé is golden brown and center feels firm when lightly tapped (35 to 40 minutes). Serve immediately. Makes about 6 servings.

◆ CHILE-CHEESE SOUFFLÉ ◆

Chiles spark a Mexican-style spin-off of the traditional French soufflé.

3½ cups (14 oz.) shredded jack cheese
3½ cups (14 oz.) shredded sharp Cheddar cheese
  1 can (7 oz.) diced green chiles
  2 medium-size tomatoes, seeded and chopped
  1 can (2¼ oz.) sliced ripe olives, drained
  ½ cup all-purpose flour
  6 eggs, separated
  1 small can (5 oz.) evaporated milk
  ½ teaspoon *each* salt and oregano leaves
  ¼ teaspoon *each* ground cumin and pepper
  ¼ teaspoon cream of tartar

In a large bowl, combine jack cheese, Cheddar cheese, chiles, tomatoes, olives, and 2 tablespoons of the flour. Toss to mix evenly. Turn mixture into a well-greased 9- by 13-inch baking dish.

Preheat oven to 300°. In a small bowl, beat egg yolks until blended. Alternately beat in remaining 6 tablespoons flour and evaporated milk. Stir in salt, oregano, cumin, and pepper.

In another large bowl, combine egg whites and cream of tartar. Beat until egg whites hold soft, moist peaks. Fold yolk mixture into egg whites;

then spoon over cheese mixture in baking dish. Bake until top is golden brown and feels firm when lightly tapped (about 1 hour). Let stand for 15 minutes before serving. Makes 10 to 12 servings.

GARLIC SOUFFLÉ

The flavor of garlic is unmistakable but surprisingly subtle in this soufflé.

  3½ **tablespoons butter or margarine**
       About 2 tablespoons grated Parmesan cheese
   3 **cloves garlic, minced or pressed**
   3 **tablespoons all-purpose flour**
       Dash *each* of ground red pepper (cayenne) and ground nutmeg
   ¼ **teaspoon *each* salt and dry mustard**
   1 **cup milk**
   1 **cup (4 oz.) shredded jack cheese**
   5 **eggs, separated**

Preheat oven to 375°. Generously butter a 2-quart soufflé dish, using ½ tablespoon of the butter. Dust buttered dish with Parmesan cheese.

Melt remaining 3 tablespoons butter in a 3-quart pan over low heat. Add garlic and cook, stirring occasionally, until garlic is soft and golden but not browned (about 5 minutes). Increase heat to medium and stir in flour, red pepper, nutmeg, salt, and mustard. Cook, stirring, until bubbly. Remove from heat and gradually stir in milk. Return to heat and cook, stirring constantly, until sauce boils and thickens. Add jack cheese and stir until melted. Remove from heat; beat in egg yolks. Set aside.

In a large bowl, beat egg whites until they hold soft, moist peaks. Thoroughly fold about ⅓ of the beaten whites into cheese sauce to lighten it; then fold in remaining whites. Pour mixture into prepared soufflé dish. Bake until top of soufflé is golden brown and center feels firm when lightly tapped (25 to 30 minutes). Serve immediately. Makes 4 or 5 servings.

APPLE & CHEDDAR CHEESE OMELET

Cinnamon and apples go together. Cheddar and apples go together. All three make this omelet fit for a holiday breakfast.

   2 **large tart apples, peeled, cored, and thinly sliced**
   1 **tablespoon lemon juice**
   ⅛ **teaspoon *each* ground nutmeg and cinnamon**
   3 **tablespoons butter or margarine**
   1 **small onion, finely chopped**
   6 **eggs**
   2 **tablespoons water**
   1 **cup (4 oz.) shredded sharp Cheddar cheese**

In a bowl, mix apples, lemon juice, nutmeg, and cinnamon. Melt 2 tablespoons of the butter in a wide frying pan over medium-high heat. Add apple mixture and onion; cook, stirring, just until apples begin to brown (about 7 minutes). Keep warm.

In a medium bowl, beat eggs and water until blended. Heat a 10- to 12-inch frying pan over medium heat. When pan is hot, add remaining 1 tablespoon butter and stir until melted. Pour egg mixture into pan. Cook just until omelet is set but still moist on top; as eggs set, lift cooked portion around edge of pan with a spatula to allow uncooked portion to flow underneath. Remove from heat. Spoon half the apple mixture and ½ cup of the cheese down center of omelet. Fold one side of omelet over filling. Slide unfolded edge onto a plate; flip folded portion over on top. Top omelet with remaining apple mixture and remaining ½ cup cheese. Makes 2 or 3 servings.

BLUE CHEESE & BASIL OMELET

The flavors of cheeses and herbs play off against each other in intriguing ways. Basil and almost any blue cheese team up in this omelet.

   8 **eggs**
   3 **tablespoons water**
   ½ **teaspoon salt**
   ¼ **teaspoon pepper**
   2 **tablespoons butter or margarine**
   1 **large clove garlic, minced or pressed**
   3 **ounces blue-veined cheese, coarsely crumbled**
   3 **tablespoons chopped fresh basil leaves or 1 tablespoon dry basil**

In a large bowl, beat eggs, water, salt, and pepper until blended.

Heat a 10-inch omelet pan or wide frying pan with sloping sides over medium-high heat. When

(Continued on next page)

pan is hot, add butter and garlic and stir until butter is melted; tilt pan so butter coats bottom and sides. Pour in egg mixture and cook just until omelet is almost set, but still moist and creamy on top; as eggs set, lift cooked portion around edges of pan with a spatula to allow uncooked portion to flow underneath. Gently shake pan to keep omelet free.

Sprinkle omelet with cheese and basil. Continue to shake pan and lift omelet edges until eggs are set and cheese is melted.

Tilt pan over a serving plate and shake pan to slide half the omelet onto plate. With a flick of the wrist, fold other half of omelet over first half. Makes 4 servings.

RED CHILE & CHEESE OMELET

A spicy sauce made from dried chiles is a delicious and colorful topping for cheese omelets. You might also use it in Corn Quesadillas with Red Chile Sauce (page 68) or as a condiment on hamburgers, tacos, or burritos.

Red Chile Sauce (recipe follows)
2 eggs
1 tablespoon water
1 to 2 teaspoons butter or margarine
1 tablespoon chopped green onion (including top)
2 to 3 tablespoons shredded Cheddar or jack cheese
Sour cream

Prepare Red Chile Sauce.

In a small bowl, beat eggs and water until blended. Heat a 6- or 7-inch omelet pan or other frying pan over medium-high heat. When pan is hot, add butter and stir until melted. Pour egg mixture into pan. Cook just until omelet is set but still moist on top; as eggs set, lift cooked portion around edges of pan with a spatula to allow uncooked portion to flow underneath. Remove from heat.

Spoon 1 to 2 tablespoons Red Chile Sauce onto half of omelet; top with onion and cheese. With a spatula, fold other half of omelet over filling. Slide omelet from pan onto a plate. Offer additional sauce and sour cream to spoon over omelet. Makes 1 serving.

Red Chile Sauce. Wipe dust off 3 ounces (8 to 12) **dried whole New Mexico or California (Anaheim) chiles** and arrange chiles on a 12- by 15-inch baking sheet. Bake in a 450° oven just until chiles smell toasted (2 to 3 minutes). Let cool. Break off and discard stems, then shake out and discard seeds.

In a 3- to 4-quart pan, combine chiles, 2½ cups **water,** 1 small **onion** (cut into chunks), and 2 cloves **garlic.** Cover and bring to a boil over high heat. Reduce heat; simmer until chiles are very soft when pierced (about 20 minutes). Remove from heat and let cool slightly.

Pour chile mixture into a blender and whirl until very smoothly puréed. (Or drain chile mixture, reserving liquid; purée solids in a food processor, then stir in liquid.) Rub purée firmly through a wire strainer to extract all pulp; discard residue. Season purée to taste with **salt.** If made ahead, cover and refrigerate for up to 1 week; freeze for longer storage. Makes about 3 cups.

ZUCCHINI-PARMESAN FRITTATA

Pictured on facing page

When zucchini season strikes, this version of Italy's overloaded omelet is a welcome way to stave off a surplus.

6 eggs
1 tablespoon water
Dash *each* of salt, pepper, and ground nutmeg
4 tablespoons butter or margarine
1 small zucchini, thinly sliced
1 small red bell pepper, seeded and cut into ½-inch squares
⅓ cup grated Parmesan cheese

In a bowl, beat eggs, water, salt, pepper, and nutmeg just until evenly blended. Set aside.

Melt 2 tablespoons of the butter in a medium-size frying pan with an ovenproof handle over medium heat. Add zucchini and bell pepper; cook, stirring, until soft. Push vegetables to one side of pan; add remaining 2 tablespoons butter and heat until melted. Stir vegetables to distribute evenly over pan bottom. Pour in egg mixture. Cook just until eggs are softly set but top of frittata is still moist; as eggs set, lift cooked portion around edge of pan with a spatula to allow uncooked portion to flow underneath.

Remove pan from heat; sprinkle cheese over frittata. Broil 6 inches below heat until cheese is melted and top of frittata is lightly browned (about 2 minutes). Cut into wedges and serve from pan. Makes 2 or 3 servings.

The frittata, Italy's hearty alternative to the omelet, is always chunky with vegetables or meat—and usually flavored with a distinctive cheese. Zucchini-Parmesan Frittata (facing page) makes an excellent luncheon main dish with salad or sliced tomatoes.

◆ CHILE-CHEESE BAKE ◆

The flavor of green chiles, cheese, and eggs go together perfectly—as in this simple-to-make variation on the familiar *chiles rellenos*.

2 cups (8 oz.) shredded sharp Cheddar cheese
2 cups (8 oz.) shredded jack cheese
2 cans (7 oz. *each*) diced green chiles
4 eggs
1½ cups milk

In a bowl, combine Cheddar cheese and jack cheese. Sprinkle about ¼ of the mixed cheeses over bottom of a greased shallow 2-quart baking dish. Top evenly with about ⅓ of the chiles. Repeat layers until all cheese and chiles have been used, finishing with a layer of cheese.

In a bowl, beat eggs until blended, then beat in milk. Pour over cheese and chiles. Bake in a 350° oven until center appears firm when dish is gently shaken (35 to 40 minutes). Let stand for about 5 minutes before serving. Makes about 6 servings.

◆ SICILIAN RICOTTA FRITTATA ◆

In Sicily proper, Pecorino would be the cheese of choice for a frittata. Parmesan is a sweeter, less salty alternative.

8 ounces ricotta cheese
6 eggs
⅓ cup grated Parmesan cheese
¼ cup finely chopped parsley
¼ teaspoon salt
Dash of pepper
2 tablespoons butter or margarine
2 tablespoons olive oil
1 clove garlic, minced or pressed

Place ricotta cheese in a medium-size bowl. Beat in eggs, one at a time. Stir in Parmesan cheese, parsley, salt, and pepper.

Melt butter in 1 tablespoon of the oil in a wide frying pan with a nonstick finish. Add garlic and cook over medium heat, stirring, until golden; *do not brown*. Pour in egg mixture and cook without stirring until egg mixture is set about ¼ inch around edge of pan. With a wide spatula, lift egg

mixture from pan sides all the way around, tipping pan to let uncooked eggs flow underneath. Continue to cook until eggs are almost set but center top of frittata is still moist and creamy.

Invert a large, round, flat heatproof plate (somewhat wider than frying pan) over frying pan. Hold pan and plate together; invert to turn frittata out onto plate. Heat remaining 1 tablespoon oil in pan; slide frittata from plate back into pan. Cook until bottom of frittata is lightly browned (about 2 minutes), then invert frittata onto a serving plate. Serve hot or at room temperature; cut into wedges to serve. Makes 3 or 4 servings.

◆ RANCHERO STRATA ◆

In texture, this strata is much like a soufflé. A simple tomato and green chile sauce gives it a mildly spicy flavor.

Tomato-Chile Sauce (recipe follows)
About ¾ pound (¾ of an oblong 1-lb. loaf) sourdough French bread
4 cups (1 lb.) shredded Cheddar cheese
1 pound bacon, crisply cooked, drained, and crumbled
6 eggs
3 cups milk
2 teaspoons dry mustard

Prepare Tomato Chile Sauce; set aside.

Cut enough bread into ½-inch-thick slices to make 2 single layers in a greased 9- by 13-inch baking dish. Arrange half the slices over bottom of dish in a single layer, cutting or overlapping slices to fit. Spread with half the sauce; sprinkle with 2 cups of the cheese and half the bacon. Repeat layers, using remaining bread, sauce, cheese, and bacon.

In a bowl, beat eggs until blended; slowly beat in milk and mustard. Pour over casserole. Cover and refrigerate for at least 8 hours or up to 24 hours. Bake, uncovered, in a 350° oven until puffed in center and hot throughout (about 55 minutes). Let stand for 20 minutes; then cut into squares to serve. Makes 8 to 10 servings.

Tomato-Chile Sauce. Pour 1 can (about 15 oz.) **tomatoes** and their liquid into a 1½- to 2-quart pan. Mash tomatoes well with a fork. Add 3 tablespoons **tomato paste**; 1 large **onion**, finely chopped; 1 clove **garlic**, minced or pressed; 1 can (4 oz.) **diced green chiles**; 1 teaspoon **oregano leaves**; and ⅛ teaspoon **ground red pepper** (cayenne). Stir well, then bring to a full boil over high heat. Use hot or cold.

Say cheese? That's easy. But pronouncing the names of all the varieties of cheese you may encounter at the supermarket or deli can be something of a challenge. Since cheeses are imported from all over the world, their names come from a variety of languages; and it's a rare individual who's fluent in more than one or two.

To help close the language gap at the cheese counter, we offer the following approximations of a number of cheese names.

Agur	Ah-GRR
Alpentop	AHL-pen-topf
Appenzeller	AH-pen-tsell-er
Banon	Bah-NONH
Bel Paese	Bell pah-EH-say
Bleu d'Auvergne	Bluh doh-VAIRN
Bleu de Bresse	Bluh duh BRESS
Bleu de Salers	Bluh duh saw-LAY
Boursault	Boor-SOH
Boursin	Boor-SANH
Brie de Coulommiers	Bree duh coo-LUM-ee-eh
Brie de Meaux	Bree duh MOH
Brie de Melun	Bree duh meh-LUNH
Brillat-Savarin	Bree-YAH Sah-vah-RANH
Bûcheron	Bew-sher-ONH
Cabicou	Cah-bee-COO
Caciocavallo	Cot-chee-oh-cah-VAHL-oh
Caciota	Cot-chee-OH-tah
Caerphilly	Car-FILL-ee
Camembert	Cahm-ahm-BEAR
Cantelet	Cahn-teh-LAY
Carré de l'Est	Cahr-RAY duh LEST
Chèvre	Shev
Chèvrefeuille	Shev-FOY
Crescenza	Creh-CHENT-za
Crottin	Craw-TANH
Crottin de Chavignol	Craw-TANH duh shah-veen-YOL
Délice de France	Day-LEASE duh frahns
Dolcelatte	Dolt-shay-LAH-tay
l'Explorateur	Lex-plor-ah-TUR
Folie du Chef	Foh-LEE dew shef
Friulano	Free-you-LAH-no
Goutu	Goo-TIU
Gratte Paille	Graht PIE

Jarlsberg	YARLS-bearg
Livarot	Lee-vah-ROH
Maroilles	Mar-WALL
Marquis de Cremembert	Mar-KEE duh crehm-ahm-BEAR
Mascarpone	Mahs-car-POH-nay
Montrachet	Monh-rah-SHAY
Montvalay	Mohn-vah-LAY
Pipo Crem'	Pea-poh CREHM
Pont l'Évêque	Ponh lay-VECK
Port du Salut	Por dew sah-LOO
Provolone Dolce	Pro-vo-LO-nay DOLT-shay
Provolone Piccante	Pro-vo-LO-nay Pea-CAHN-tay
Reblochon	Reh-bloh-SHONH
Revidoux	Reh-vee-DOO
Rondeau	Ronh-DOH
St. André	Sanh tawn-DRAY
St. Chevrier	Sanh shev-ree-EH
St. Félice	Sanh fay-LEASE
St. Honoré	Sanh tawn-oh-RAY
St. Marcellin	Sanh mar-seh-LANH
St. Nectaire	Sanh Neck-TARE
St. Otho	Sanh Toh-TOH
St. Paulin	Sanh poh-LANH
Sbrinz	Ssbrints
Steiermark	SHTY-er-mark
Stracchino	Straw-KEE-noh
Taleggio	Tah-LEG-ee-oh
Taupinière	Toh-peen-ee-AIR
Tome	Tohm
Tomme de Savoie	Tohm-duh sah-VWAH
Tybo	TEW-boh
Valencay	Vah-lawn-SAY
Vecchia Baita	VECK-kee-ya BAY-tah
Weisslacker Bierkäse	VICE-lahk-er BEER-cay-zuh

Bake these individual Almond-crusted Watercress Tarts (facing page)
to serve as a brunch or picnic entrée. They're delicious hot or cold,
with fresh fruits (as shown) or thinly sliced ham or turkey.

PIES, QUICHES & CRÊPES

Pies, quiches, and crêpes, in all their diversity, offer imaginative cooks almost unlimited opportunity to explore the flavors of cheese.

ALMOND-CRUSTED WATERCRESS TARTS

Pictured on facing page

Sweet nuts contrast with peppery cress in these little brunch or picnic tarts; any of the Swiss cheeses can harmonize the flavors of crust and filling. For variation, you might make the crust with pecans, walnuts, or hazelnuts in place of almonds.

> Almond Short Pastry (recipe follows)
> 1 cup (4 oz.) shredded Gruyère or Swiss cheese
> 2 tablespoons butter or margarine
> ¼ teaspoon dry tarragon
> 2 cups lightly packed watercress sprigs
> 3 eggs
> ½ cup half-and-half or light cream
> 1 teaspoon Dijon mustard
> ½ teaspoon salt
> ⅛ teaspoon ground nutmeg

Prepare and chill pastry, then divide into 6 equal portions. On a lightly floured board, roll out each portion and fit into a 4-inch-diameter, 1-inch-deep tart pan. Trim edges of each pastry shell flush with pan rim. Place pans on a large baking sheet; sprinkle cheese evenly into pastry shells.

Melt butter with tarragon in a wide frying pan over medium heat. Add watercress; stir just until coated with butter and slightly wilted (30 seconds to 1 minute).

Remove pan from heat and transfer watercress mixture to a blender or food processor; add eggs, half-and-half, mustard, salt, and nutmeg. Whirl until watercress is puréed. Pour purée evenly over cheese in pastry shells.

Bake in a 450° oven for 10 minutes. Reduce oven heat to 350° and continue to bake until tarts are golden brown all over and a knife inserted in centers comes out clean (18 to 20 more minutes). Place on a rack and let cool for about 5 minutes,

then carefully lift tarts out of pans and place on a serving plate. Makes 6 tarts.

Almond Short Pastry. In a bowl, stir together 1 cup **all-purpose flour,** ⅛ teaspoon **salt,** and ⅓ cup finely ground **almonds.** Using a pastry blender or 2 knives, cut in ¼ cup firm **butter** until fat particles are the size of peas. Add 2 tablespoons chilled **solid vegetable shortening;** cut in until mixture resembles fine crumbs. Sprinkle in 2 to 4 tablespoons **cold water,** mixing with a fork just until dough clings together. Gather dough into a ball with your hands. Wrap in plastic wrap and refrigerate for 1 hour.

NO-CRUST VEGETABLE & CHEESE PIE

Two mild, soft, meltable cheeses—ricotta and jack—help give this crustless pie its tender texture and subtle flavor. If you like, substitute diced cooked sausage or another meat for the ham.

> ⅓ cup butter or margarine
> ¼ pound mushrooms, thinly sliced
> 1 clove garlic, minced or pressed
> 1 small zucchini, thinly sliced
> 1 cup diced cooked ham
> 1 package (10 oz.) frozen chopped spinach, thawed
> 4 eggs
> 1 pound ricotta cheese
> 1 cup (4 oz.) shredded jack cheese
> ½ teaspoon dill weed
> ¼ teaspoon pepper

Melt butter in a wide frying pan over medium heat. Add mushrooms, garlic, and zucchini; cook, stirring, just until mushrooms are soft (about 3 minutes). Stir in ham; cook for 1 more minute. Remove from heat and set aside.

Drain spinach well, then place in a small colander and press out as much water as possible. Set aside.

In a large bowl, beat eggs until blended. Add spinach, ricotta cheese, jack cheese, dill weed, pepper, and mushroom mixture. Mix well. Pour into a greased 10-inch pie pan or quiche pan. Bake in a 325° oven until center of pie feels firm when lightly touched (35 to 40 minutes).

Let pie cool for 10 minutes, then cut into wedges and serve hot. Or let cool completely and serve at room temperature. Makes about 6 main-dish servings.

SPINACH & RICOTTA PIE

Perfect for lunch or an informal supper, this hearty two-crust pie features three cheeses. The ricotta contributes to the pie's silky texture, the Parmesan adds nutty flavor, and the Swiss helps hold everything together.

Flaky Pastry (page 45)
1 package (10 oz.) frozen chopped spinach, thawed
1 pound ricotta cheese
¼ pound mushrooms, chopped
½ cup shredded Swiss cheese
½ cup grated Parmesan cheese
¼ pound thinly sliced pepperoni
¼ cup finely chopped onion
2 teaspoons prepared mustard
½ teaspoon oregano leaves
¼ teaspoon salt
Dash of pepper
1 egg
Tomato Sauce (recipe follows)

Prepare Flaky Pastry as directed on page 45, but omit caraway seeds or chili powder.

Drain spinach thoroughly; place in a colander and press out as much water as possible. In a bowl, combine spinach, ricotta cheese, mushrooms, Swiss cheese, Parmesan cheese, pepperoni, onion, mustard, oregano, salt, and pepper. Mix well, then beat in egg. Set aside.

On a lightly floured board, roll out half the pastry and fit into a 9-inch pie pan. Trim pastry extending beyond pan rim to leave a ½-inch overhang. Spoon filling evenly into pastry-lined pan. Roll out remaining pastry and place on pie; seal and flute edges. Prick top in several places with a fork to allow steam to escape.

Bake in a 425° oven until crust is browned (about 25 minutes). Let cool for about 10 minutes. Meanwhile, prepare Tomato Sauce.

To serve, cut pie into wedges; pass hot Tomato Sauce at the table to accompany pie. Makes 6 main-dish servings.

Tomato Sauce. In a small pan, stir together 1 can (15 oz.) **tomato sauce,** ½ teaspoon **garlic salt,** a dash of **pepper,** and 1 teaspoon **Italian herb seasoning** or ¼ teaspoon *each* dry basil, oregano leaves, thyme leaves, and marjoram leaves. Place over medium heat and cook, stirring, until bubbly. Keep hot until ready to serve.

QUICHE LORRAINE

Cooked bacon is the signature ingredient of quiche Lorraine, but a flavorful Gruyère is almost as vital a part of the traditional recipe.

Pastry Dough (recipe follows)
10 slices bacon, crisply cooked, drained, and crumbled
1¼ cups (about 5 oz.) diced Gruyère or Swiss cheese (¼-inch cubes)
4 eggs
1¼ cups whipping cream, half-and-half, or light cream
½ cup milk
Freshly grated or ground nutmeg

Prepare and chill Pastry Dough. On a lightly floured board, roll out dough and fit into a 10-inch quiche pan or pie pan. (Dough tears easily, but does not toughen with handling; pinch any tears together to rejoin.) If using a quiche pan, trim pastry flush with pan rim. If using a pie pan, trim pastry extending beyond rim to leave a ½-inch overhang. Fold overhang under itself and press lightly to seal; then flute edge of crust.

Scatter bacon in pastry shell; sprinkle with cheese. Beat eggs, cream, and milk just until blended; pour into pastry shell. Sprinkle with nutmeg.

Bake on lowest rack of a 350° oven until quiche is slightly puffed and appears set when pan is gently shaken (about 1 hour). Let cool for 10 minutes, then serve. Or place on a rack, let cool completely, and serve at room temperature. Makes 8 to 10 first-course servings or 6 main-dish servings.

Pastry Dough. In a bowl, stir together 1½ cups **all-purpose flour** and ¼ teaspoon **salt.** Using a pastry blender or 2 knives, cut in ½ cup (¼ lb.) plus 2 tablespoons firm **butter** or margarine until mixture resembles fine crumbs. Lightly beat 1 **egg;** add to flour mixture and stir with a fork until dough holds together. Gather dough into a ball with your hands. Wrap in plastic wrap and refrigerate for 1 hour.

LEEK & HAM QUICHE

Quiche Lorraine has numerous variations, including this one for winter. In spring, try substituting shrimp and asparagus for the ham and leeks. (Use ¾ pound asparagus, sliced and steamed or boiled, and ½ pound small cooked shrimp.)

Flaky Butter Pastry (recipe follows)
2 leeks (about 1 lb. *total*)
2 tablespoons butter or margarine
1½ cups (6 oz.) shredded Swiss cheese
1 cup finely diced cooked ham
4 eggs
1 cup half-and-half or light cream
¼ teaspoon *each* salt and dry mustard
Pinch *each* of ground nutmeg and white pepper

Prepare Flaky Butter Pastry. On a floured board, roll out pastry and fit into a 1½-inch-deep 9-inch pie pan. Trim pastry extending beyond pan rim to leave a ½-inch overhang. Fold overhang under itself and press lightly to seal; flute edge of crust. Cut a circle of foil to fit in pie shell; line shell with foil circle. Half-fill foil-lined shell with raw beans or pie weights. Bake in a 425° oven for 10 minutes. Lift off foil and beans; bake for 5 more minutes. Place on a rack. Reduce oven heat to 350°.

Trim and discard ends and tops from leeks, leaving about 3 inches of dark green leaves. Discard tough outer leaves. Split leeks lengthwise; rinse well, then thinly slice crosswise. Melt butter in a medium-size frying pan over medium heat. Add leeks and cook, stirring often, until bright green and tender-crisp to bite (3 to 5 minutes).

Sprinkle ¾ cup of the cheese into pastry shell; evenly top with leeks and ham. In a bowl, beat eggs, half-and-half, salt, mustard, nutmeg, and white pepper until blended. Pour over leek mixture. Sprinkle with remaining ¾ cup cheese.

Bake until a knife inserted in center comes out clean (40 to 45 minutes). Let stand for 10 minutes, then serve. Makes 6 main-dish servings.

Flaky Butter Pastry. Prepare **Pastry Dough** (page 64), but reduce flour to 1 cup and use only 6 tablespoons butter or margarine.

◆ HAM & CHEESE CRÊPES ◆

A traditional Brittany crêpe pan is big—10 to 14 inches across. If you don't have this special pan, an 8- to 10-inch frying pan will do.

3 eggs
1 cup all-purpose flour
1½ cups milk
About 6 tablespoons butter or margarine
About ½ pound thinly sliced cooked ham
3 cups (12 oz.) shredded Swiss or Gruyère cheese

In a blender or food processor, combine eggs and flour. Whirl until blended. Scrape down sides of blender container or processor work bowl; add milk and whirl until smooth.

Place a Brittany crêpe pan or an 8- to 10-inch frying pan over medium-high heat. Add about 2 teaspoons butter. When butter is melted, tilt pan to coat bottom.

Measure about ¼ cup batter for a pan with an 8-inch base, about ⅓ cup for a pan with a 10- to 12-inch base, and a scant ½ cup for a pan with a 14-inch base. Remove hot pan from heat, pour in batter, and quickly tilt pan to coat bottom evenly. Return pan to heat; cook just until surface of crêpe feels dry and edges are golden brown. Run a wide spatula around edges of crêpe to loosen; then flip pan over to turn crêpe out onto a plate.

Repeat with remaining batter, adding more butter to pan as needed. Stack crêpes as they are completed. If made ahead, place wax paper between crêpes, wrap airtight, and refrigerate for up to 1 week. Freeze for longer storage. Bring crêpes to room temperature before separating.

To assemble crêpes, place on a flat surface, browned side down. Place an equal amount of ham in center of each crêpe; sprinkle ham evenly with cheese. Fold in sides of each crêpe to cover filling, then fold in ends and turn crêpe over. Arrange folded crêpes, seam side down, in a single layer in a greased baking dish. Cover and bake in a 375° oven until cheese is melted and crêpes are heated through (about 25 minutes). Makes about 8 main-dish servings.

◆ APPLE & BRIE CRÊPES ◆

Crisp apples and soft Brie are a classic combination, used here as filling in a crêpe "sandwich."

8 Basic Crêpes (recipe on page 66)
8 ounces firm-ripe Brie or Camembert, thinly sliced
2 small Red Delicious apples, cored, quartered, and thinly sliced
2 tablespoons butter or margarine
½ cup walnut halves or pieces

Prepare Basic Crêpes. Place 4 of the crêpes, slightly apart, in a single layer on two 10- by 15-inch baking sheets. Arrange cheese and apples evenly over crêpes; top with remaining 4 crêpes. Melt butter in a small pan; stir in walnuts. Sprinkle nut mixture evenly over crêpes. Bake, uncovered, in a 425° oven until cheese is melted (about 5 minutes). With a

(Continued on next page)

wide spatula, transfer each crêpe "sandwich" to a warm plate. Serve at once. Makes 4 main-dish servings.

Basic Crêpes. In a blender or food processor, combine 1 cup **milk,** 3 **eggs,** and ⅔ cup **all-purpose flour.** Whirl until smooth.

Place a 6- or 7-inch crêpe pan or other flat-bottomed frying pan over medium heat. Melt ¼ teaspoon **butter** or margarine in pan; swirl to coat surface.

Stir batter thoroughly. Pour about 2 tablespoons of the batter into pan all at once; quickly tilt pan so batter flows over entire flat surface. Cook until surface of crêpe feels dry and edges are lightly browned. Turn crêpe and cook until lightly browned on other side. Remove from pan and place on a plate.

Repeat with remaining batter to make 15 to 17 more crêpes, adding ¼ teaspoon **butter** or margarine to pan before making each crêpe. Stack crêpes as they are completed. If made ahead, place wax paper between crêpes, wrap airtight, and refrigerate for up to 1 week. Freeze for longer storage. Bring crêpes to room temperature before separating. Makes 16 to 18 crêpes.

◆ MUSHROOM-CHEESE ◆ CRÊPES

Pictured on facing page

In addition to melting well, Swiss cheeses add just the right understated flavor to a crêpe having other subtly flavored ingredients.

12	Whole Wheat Crêpes (recipe follows)
	Béchamel Sauce (recipe follows)
3	tablespoons butter or margarine
1	pound mushrooms, thinly sliced
1	shallot or green onion (including top), finely chopped
1	small clove garlic, minced or pressed
¼	teaspoon dry tarragon
1	tablespoon dry sherry
½	cup whipping cream
1½	cups (6 oz.) shredded Gruyère or Swiss cheese
	Freshly grated or ground nutmeg
	Tomato wedges (optional)

Prepare crêpes and set aside. Prepare Béchamel Sauce and set aside.

Melt butter in a wide frying pan over medium-high heat; add mushrooms, shallot, and garlic. Cook, stirring often, until mushrooms are lightly browned and liquid has evaporated (8 to 10 minutes). Lift about ¼ cup of the mushroom mixture from pan and reserve for garnish. Sprinkle tarragon over remaining mixture; remove from heat and stir in sherry and half the Béchamel Sauce. Spoon an equal amount of filling down center of each crêpe; roll to enclose. Place filled crêpes, seam side down, in a single layer in a lightly greased 9- by 13-inch baking dish. (At this point, you may cover and refrigerate filled crêpes, reserved mushroom mixture, and sauce until next day.)

Stir cream into remaining Béchamel Sauce. Place over medium heat; heat, stirring often, until sauce is heated through. Pour evenly over crêpes, sprinkle with cheese, and dust lightly with nutmeg. Bake, uncovered, in a 425° oven until lightly browned and bubbly (12 to 15 minutes; 20 minutes if refrigerated). Spoon reserved mushroom mixture onto crêpes. Garnish with tomato wedges, if desired. Makes about 4 main-dish servings.

Whole Wheat Crêpes. In a blender or food processor, combine 1 cup **milk,** 3 **eggs,** 1 tablespoon **salad oil,** ¾ cup **whole wheat flour** (not stoneground), and ⅛ teaspoon **salt.** Whirl until smooth. Cover and refrigerate for 1 hour.

Heat a 6- or 7-inch crêpe pan or other flat-bottomed frying pan over medium heat. Pour in about ¼ teaspoon **salad oil** and swirl to coat surface. When pan is sizzling hot (test with a few drops of water), stir batter thoroughly. Then pour about 2 tablespoons of the batter into pan all at once; quickly tilt pan so batter flows over entire flat surface. Cook until surface of crêpe feels dry and edges are lightly browned. Turn crêpe and cook until lightly browned on other side. Remove from pan and place on a plate.

Repeat with remaining batter, adding a little oil as needed to prevent crêpes from sticking. Stack crêpes as they are completed. If made ahead, place wax paper between crêpes, wrap airtight, and refrigerate for up to 3 days; freeze for longer storage. Bring crêpes to room temperature before separating. Makes 16 to 18 crêpes.

Béchamel Sauce. Melt ¼ cup **butter** or margarine in a 1½- to 2-quart pan over medium heat. Stir in ¼ cup **all-purpose flour,** ¼ teaspoon **salt,** and a dash of **ground red pepper** (cayenne). Cook, stirring, until bubbly. Remove from heat and gradually stir in 2 cups **milk.** Return to heat and cook, stirring constantly, until sauce boils and thickens. In a medium-size bowl, beat 3 **egg yolks.** Slowly pour in some of the hot sauce, stirring constantly; then stir egg mixture back into sauce. Continue to cook, stirring, just until sauce thickens (about 1 minute); do not let sauce boil.

The French are ingenious at finding ways to eat fine cheeses.
In these Mushroom-Cheese Crêpes (facing page), a Gruyère-based filling is enclosed
in a whole wheat wrapper, then covered with creamy béchamel sauce.

67

◆ CORN QUESADILLAS WITH RED CHILE SAUCE ◆

Quesadillas—cheese-filled tortillas—are staple appetizers in Mexican cookery. The chile sauce makes them anything but bland.

> **Red Chile Sauce (page 58)**
> 1 **cup (4 oz.) shredded jack cheese**
> 1 **cup (4 oz.) shredded Cheddar cheese**
> **About 4 tablespoons butter or margarine**
> 8 **corn tortillas,** *each* **6 to 7 inches in diameter**
> **Fresh cilantro (coriander) sprigs (optional)**

Prepare Red Chile Sauce and set aside.

In a bowl, combine jack cheese and Cheddar cheese. Melt 2 tablespoons butter in a 10- to 12-inch frying pan over medium heat. Place one tortilla in pan; when tortilla is slightly warm, place ¼ cup of the mixed cheeses on half of tortilla. With a spatula, fold other half of tortilla over cheese to shape quesadilla. Repeat with more tortillas and cheese to make 1 or 2 more quesadillas—as many as will fit in pan without crowding. Cook quesadillas, turning as needed, until lightly browned on both sides (about 1 minute). Remove from pan and keep warm. Repeat with remaining tortillas and cheese, adding more butter to pan as needed to prevent sticking.

To serve, spoon about 2 tablespoons sauce onto each quesadilla. If desired, garnish with cilantro. Makes 3 or 4 servings.

◆ QUICK QUESADILLAS ◆

Peppers and taco sauces offer quick and easy ways to spice up plain quesadillas. For a heartier snack, include a few slices of meat.

> 4 **flour tortillas,** *each* **about 8 inches in diameter**
> 2 **cups (8 oz.) shredded Cheddar, jack, or Swiss cheese**
> ¼ **cup canned diced green chiles (optional)**

Cover half of each tortilla with cheese to within ½ inch of edge. Sprinkle with chiles, if desired. Fold other half of each tortilla over cheese; place on a baking sheet. Bake in a 450° oven until cheese is melted and tortilla is lightly browned (about 5 minutes). Serve immediately. Makes 2 to 4 servings.

SPICY QUESADILLAS

Follow directions for **Quick Quesadillas,** but drizzle 1 tablespoon **prepared taco sauce** over cheese on each tortilla before folding.

MEAT QUESADILLAS

Follow directions for **Quick Quesadillas,** but use only 1 cup (4 oz.) cheese and add 1 slice (or about ¼ cup diced) **cooked chicken,** turkey, or beef to each tortilla.

◆ CHEESE ENCHILADAS ◆

In this hearty Mexican main dish, mild Cheddar adds a welcome bit of flavor as a stand-in for a Mexican firm cheese.

> **Cheese Filling (recipe follows)**
> **Salad oil**
> 12 **corn tortillas,** *each* **6 to 7 inches in diameter**
> 1 **can (7 oz.) green chile salsa**
> 2 **cups (8 oz.) shredded mild Cheddar cheese**
> **About 1 cup shredded iceberg lettuce**
> 2 **medium-size tomatoes, thinly sliced**
> 3 **green onions (including tops), thinly sliced**

Prepare Cheese Filling; set aside.

Into a small frying pan, pour oil to a depth of ¼ inch; heat over medium heat. When oil is hot, dip in one tortilla; cook just until limp and beginning to blister (a few seconds). *Do not fry until firm or crisp.* Remove with tongs; drain briefly. Repeat with remaining 11 tortillas, adding more oil as needed.

Spread ⅓ of the salsa evenly in a 9- by 13-inch baking dish. Spoon about ⅓ cup filling down center of each tortilla; roll to enclose. Arrange tortillas in dish, seam side down. Cover with remaining salsa and sprinkle with shredded cheese. (At this point, you may cover and refrigerate until next day.)

Bake, uncovered, in a 375° oven until bubbly and heated through—about 20 minutes. (If refrigerated, bake for 15 minutes covered; then uncover and bake for about 15 more minutes.) Garnish enchiladas with lettuce, tomatoes, and onions. Makes 6 main-dish servings.

Cheese Filling. In a bowl, stir together 3 cups **large curd cottage cheese,** 1 cup (4 oz.) shredded **mild Cheddar cheese,** 1½ cups sliced **green onions** (including tops), and ¼ teaspoon **oregano leaves.**

Salad and cheese form a natural partnership. Perhaps the most familiar example for Americans is green salad with a blue cheese dressing, but several other combinations come quickly to mind: cubed or shredded Cheddar or Swiss in any of the hundreds of variations on chef's salad; crumbled feta in Mediterranean-style salads; and cottage cheese and lettuce, with or without fruit as a third element.

Most of Europe offers another possibility—that of serving green salad and cheese side by side, sometimes to finish the meal, sometimes as an interlude before a sweet dessert. Used in this fashion, the cheese usually comes to the table on a separate tray; guests are invited to cut as much as they wish to put alongside their salads.

Both of the green salads on this page make good companions to various cheeses. Below are some of the choices to consider.

Blue cheeses. If a blue can be mixed into a creamy dressing or crumbled straight into a salad, it can also be served sliced alongside the same salad. (See page 12 for a selection of blue cheeses.)

Goat cheeses. The tangy taste of goat's milk in fresh chèvres goes well with greens—and makes an excellent counterpoint to any sweet dessert that might follow. Herb- or pepper-flavored chèvres are often especially appropriate. (See page 21 for notes on goat cheeses.)

Fresh cheeses. Many of these contribute the same soft texture as a chèvre, but they have sweeter flavors that harmonize with a dessert rather than providing a counterpoint to it. Cream cheese is the premier example, with Boursault not far behind. Herb-flavored Boursin is also a natural in this role.

Soft-ripened double and triple creams. In combination with a salad, these richer kin to Brie and Camembert provide a perfect grand finale for a meal. (See page 15.)

Monastery and other semisoft cheeses. The stronger members of this group can be too much, but milder types such as Bel Paese and St. Paulin work well with salads. (See page 26.)

Firm and grating cheeses. Parmesan grates over greens but is too hard to slice. But Asiago, dry jack, and kasseri are grating cheeses that may also be sliced. And Swiss, Cheddar, Edam, Gouda, and most of the other firm cheeses are good company, as well.

SHALLOT & GREENS SALAD

¼ cup minced shallots
6 tablespoons olive oil or salad oil
3 tablespoons red wine vinegar
1 tablespoon Dijon mustard
2 cups lightly packed watercress leaves
2 medium-size heads butter lettuce, broken into bite-size pieces
Salt

In a small bowl, stir together shallots, oil, vinegar, and mustard. Combine watercress and lettuce in a salad bowl. Pour dressing over greens; season to taste with salt. Toss lightly. Makes 4 to 6 servings.

THREE GREENS SALAD

1 large clove garlic, cut in half
6 tablespoons olive oil or salad oil
2½ tablespoons red wine vinegar
2 cups *each* lightly packed bite-size pieces butter lettuce and red leaf lettuce
2 cups lightly packed small inner romaine lettuce leaves
Salt and freshly ground pepper

In a glass measure, combine garlic and oil; let stand for 30 minutes. Discard garlic. Stir vinegar into oil. Combine greens in a salad bowl. Pour dressing over greens; season to taste with salt and pepper. Toss lightly. Makes 4 to 6 servings.

A fondue served right from the barbecue, Mexican-style Grilled Cheese
(page 72) features shrimp, tomatoes, jalapeño peppers,
and any smooth soft cheese. Crisp tortillas make perfect dippers.

FONDUES & RAREBITS

Fondues and rarebits (or rabbits) both grew out of long, chill winters that called for warmth not only in food, but among friends. Fondues, especially, are still among the most sociable of dishes.

◆ CHUNKY CHEDDAR FONDUE ◆

Cheddar cheese, tomatoes, and chiles star in this spicy departure from traditional cheese fondue. Another difference here is the un-Swiss assortment of dippers.

- 3 tablespoons butter or margarine
- 1 medium-size onion, chopped
- 1 can (about 8 oz.) stewed tomatoes
- 1 can (4 oz.) whole green chiles, seeded and chopped
- ¼ teaspoon oregano leaves
- 4 cups (1 lb.) shredded Cheddar cheese
  Assorted crisp raw vegetables (suggestions follow)
  Firm French bread cubes, tortilla chips, or breadsticks

Melt butter in a wide frying pan over medium heat. Add onion and cook, stirring occasionally, until lightly browned. Stir in tomatoes (break up with a spoon) and their liquid, chiles, and oregano. Reduce heat and simmer, uncovered, for 5 minutes. Add a handful of cheese and stir with a wooden spoon until melted. Repeat with remaining cheese.

To serve, transfer to a fondue pot or chafing dish and adjust heat source to keep fondue hot. (Or serve in frying pan, reheating as necessary. To reheat, place over medium heat; stir until cheese is melted.) Use vegetables and bread cubes as dippers. If desired, offer fondue forks or bamboo skewers to spear bread cubes and smaller vegetable pieces. Makes 8 to 10 appetizer servings or 3 or 4 main-dish servings.

Assorted vegetables. Choose 3 or more from the following: **carrot** sticks or whole baby carrots; **celery** sticks; **green or red bell pepper** strips; **zucchini** slices; **green onions; cauliflowerets; mushrooms** (quartered, if large).

◆ CHEESE FONDUE ◆

Pictured on page 1

Though a classic fondue can be made with a single cheese, the Swiss themselves use two—both Swiss and Gruyère—to give the dish a more complex flavor. To ensure a smooth fondue, keep the heat just low enough during both cooking and serving. If the heat is too low, the cheese will not melt smoothly—but if it's too high, the cheese becomes stringy.

A traditional fondue pot of heavy metal or heat-resistant earthenware is ideal for one-step cooking and serving.

- 2 cups (8 oz.) shredded imported Swiss cheese (Emmenthaler)
- 2 cups (8 oz.) shredded Gruyère or Samsoe cheese
- 1½ tablespoons cornstarch
- 1 teaspoon dry mustard
  Freshly ground pepper and ground nutmeg
- 1 clove garlic, cut in half
- 1½ cups dry white wine
- 1 tablespoon lemon juice
- 2 tablespoons kirsch (optional)
  Firm French bread cubes

In a large bowl, toss Swiss cheese and Gruyère cheese with cornstarch and mustard; season to taste with pepper and nutmeg.

Rub cut sides of garlic over sides and bottom of a fondue pot or 2-quart pan. Discard garlic. Add wine and lemon juice, place over medium heat, and heat until bubbles rise slowly to the surface. Add a handful of the cheese mixture and stir with a wooden spoon until melted. Repeat with remaining cheese mixture. Adjust heat so fondue is just simmering. If desired, stir in kirsch, a tablespoon at a time.

If fondue is too thick, add a small amount of warmed (never cold) wine and stir in completely. If fondue separates, mix 1 tablespoon cornstarch, 1 teaspoon lemon juice, and ¼ cup wine; warm slightly and stir into fondue.

Place fondue over heat source and adjust heat so fondue keeps bubbling *slowly*. Offer fondue forks or bamboo skewers to spear bread for dipping. Makes 12 appetizer servings or 4 main-dish servings.

DUTCH GOUDA FONDUE

Follow directions for **Cheese Fondue,** but substitute 4 cups (1 lb.) shredded **Gouda cheese** for imported Swiss and Gruyère cheeses.

◆ BRIE FONDUE ◆

Brie melts into a distinctively flavorful fondue that's more liquid and less stringy than the traditional Swiss cheese version.

- **1 whole, firm Brie cheese (2 lbs.)**
- **1 to 1½ pounds mild Italian sausages**
- **2 or 3 large red or green bell peppers**
- **About 24 breadsticks**

Place cheese in top of a 9- to 10-inch chafing dish. Heat, stirring occasionally, until melted (15 to 20 minutes). Reduce heat to medium-low.

While cheese is melting, thickly slice sausages. Cook in a wide frying pan over medium heat until browned; drain. Seed bell peppers and cut lengthwise into ½- to 1-inch-wide strips.

Scoop up melted cheese with sausage slices, bell pepper strips, and breadsticks. Makes about 24 appetizer servings or about 6 main-dish servings.

◆ CREAMY PARMESAN FONDUE ◆

Cream cheese or Neufchâtel blends smoothly with grated Parmesan in this easy and uncomplicated fondue.

- **2 large packages (8 oz. *each*) cream cheese or Neufchâtel cheese**
- **About 2 cups milk**
- **2 small cloves garlic, minced or pressed**
- **About 1½ cups (about 7½ oz.) grated Parmesan cheese**
- **Salt**
- **Freshly ground pepper or thinly sliced green onion (including top)**
- **Firm French bread cubes**

Place cream cheese in top of a double boiler; set over simmering water. As cheese melts, gradually add 2 cups of the milk, stirring until mixture is smooth. Add garlic and Parmesan cheese; stir until cheese is melted and sauce is thickened. Season to taste with salt; if needed, add more milk to thin to good dipping consistency.

To serve, transfer fondue to a ceramic fondue pot or a chafing dish and adjust heat source to keep fondue hot. Sprinkle with pepper. Offer fondue forks or bamboo skewers to spear bread for dipping. Makes 12 to 16 appetizer servings.

◆ MEXICAN-STYLE GRILLED CHEESE ◆

Pictured on page 70

The Mexican version of fondue uses a smooth, soft cheese; jack, American Münster, and fontina-types come closest to Mexico's *queso asadero*.

- **24 corn tortillas**
- **Salad oil**
- **1½ tablespoons olive oil**
- **1 large onion, chopped**
- **2 large tomatoes, seeded and coarsely chopped**
- **¼ teaspoon ground cinnamon**
- **7 to 9 small fresh or canned jalapeño peppers**
- **Salt**
- **2 pounds mild cheese, such as jack, Münster, fontina, Edam, or Gouda**
- **1 cup small cooked shrimp**

Cut tortillas into quarters. Into a deep 2- to 3-quart pan, pour salad oil to a depth of 2 inches. Heat over medium-high heat to 375°F on a deep-frying thermometer. Add tortilla pieces, 6 to 8 at a time, and cook until crisp and golden brown (about 1 minute). Lift out with a slotted spoon; drain on paper towels. If made ahead, let cool, then store airtight at room temperature for up to 2 days. To reheat, spread in a single layer on large baking sheets. Bake in a 400° oven until crisp (about 10 minutes).

Heat olive oil in a wide frying pan over medium-high heat. Add onion and cook, stirring often, until soft (about 10 minutes). Add tomatoes and cinnamon. Increase heat to high; cook, stirring, for 1 minute. Chop 4 to 6 of the peppers; stir into tomato mixture. Season to taste with salt.

Trim any wax coating from cheese, then cut cheese into ¼-inch-thick slices. Arrange in an 8- to 10-inch metal pan or heatproof ceramic dish at least 1½ inches deep, overlapping slices to cover pan bottom and extend up just to pan edges. (At this point, you may cover and let stand for up to 4 hours.) Just before heating, spoon tomato mixture over cheese in a 6-inch circle. Top with shrimp and reserved peppers.

Place pan on a grill 4 to 6 inches above a partial bed of medium coals; keep a section of fire grate empty so there's a cool area on grill. Let cheese melt, checking frequently to be sure cheese isn't scorching on bottom by pushing down into center of dish with the tip of a knife. If cheese is getting hot too fast, move it to cool area of grill. To eat, scoop melted cheese mixture onto tortillas. Makes 12 to 16 appetizer servings.

CHILE CON QUESO

Mellow Cheddar cheese helps temper the heat of green chiles in this chunky Mexican fondue.

- 2 tablespoons salad oil
- 2 medium-size onions, chopped
- 2 cans (7 oz. *each*) diced green chiles
- 1 small can (5 oz.) evaporated milk
- 2 cups (8 oz.) shredded jack or mild Cheddar cheese
  Salt
  Crisp raw vegetables

Heat oil in a 10- to 12-inch frying pan over medium-low heat. Add onions; cook, stirring occasionally, until very soft. Add chiles and simmer, stirring, until juices have evaporated (about 5 minutes). Stir in evaporated milk and simmer gently, stirring, until slightly thickened (about 4 minutes). Remove from heat and let cool for about 2 minutes; then stir in cheese. Cover until cheese is melted. Stir; season to taste with salt. Serve hot, with vegetables for dipping. Makes 12 appetizer servings.

RACLETTE

Now here is romance—a fireplace, a bottle of wine, and a tasty cheese set where it can melt. Raclette (from the French *racler*, "to scrape") is even simpler and more casual than Switzerland's other great tradition, fondue.

- Marinated Onions (recipe follows)
- 3 pounds very small new potatoes
  About 2 cups small sweet pickles
- 1 large chunk (2 to 3 lbs.) raclette, jack, fontina, Gruyère, Samsoe, or Swiss cheese

Prepare onions. Scrub potatoes and place in a pan; pour in boiling water to cover. Cover and boil until tender when pierced (about 20 minutes). Drain off most of water. Set potatoes, covered, next to fire or on a warming tray to keep warm during the meal. Meanwhile, arrange onions and pickles in separate serving dishes; have ready to serve. Trim any wax coating from cheese.

To make raclette at a fireplace, place cheese chunk in a shallow pan somewhat larger than cheese. Make just one portion of raclette (or what you plan to eat at once) at a time. Set pan on hearth and push wide surface of cheese in close to fire. When surface of cheese begins to melt, scrape it off and spoon onto a bit of hot potato along with onions and pickles. Pull cheese away from heat until you are ready for the next serving; diners can tend to their own needs.

To make raclette using a broiler, cut cheese into ½-inch-thick slices. Arrange slices, side by side, to cover bottom of a shallow pan such as a pie pan. Broil about 4 inches below heat until cheese is melted and bubbling; serve at once. Have ready as many pans of cheese as you will need; broil when ready to serve. Eat cheese with potatoes, onions, and pickles as directed above.

Makes 12 to 18 appetizer servings or 6 to 9 main-dish servings.

Marinated Onions. Thinly slice 2 medium-size **mild white onions.** Place in a bowl and mix in ⅓ cup **white wine vinegar,** ½ teaspoon **salt,** and 1½ teaspoons **sugar.** Cover and refrigerate for at least 1 hour, stirring occasionally.

WELSH RAREBIT

This old Welsh dish remains one of the finest of the world's variations on the open-faced sandwich with melted cheese.

- 1 tablespoon butter or margarine
- 1 tablespoon Worcestershire
- ½ teaspoon *each* dry mustard and paprika
  Dash of ground red pepper (cayenne)
- ½ cup beer or ale
- 2 cups (8 oz.) shredded Cheddar cheese
- 4 to 8 slices toast
  Accompaniments (optional; suggestions follow)

Place butter, Worcestershire, mustard, paprika, and red pepper in a heavy 2- to 3-quart pan over medium-low heat (or place in top of a double boiler over simmering water). Stir until butter is melted. Add beer and continue to cook, stirring, until mixture is warm to the touch; do not boil. Add a handful of cheese and stir with a wooden spoon until melted. Repeat with remaining cheese. To serve, pour cheese mixture over toast; offer accompaniments, if desired. Makes about 4 servings.

Accompaniments. Choose from thinly sliced **boiled or smoked ham,** roast beef, or roast turkey; crisply cooked **bacon slices;** or thinly sliced **tomato** or onion.

These three sauces demonstrate both the versatility and variety of cheese in cooking. Fonduta can be used as a fondue or poured over vegetables or meats. The Cheddar and Mornay sauces use different cheeses to give new flavors to versatile white sauce, so often a component of casseroles, sauced crêpes, and au gratins.

FONDUTA

Pictured on facing page

- 4 **egg yolks**
- 1 **cup milk**
- 3 **cups (12 oz.) finely shredded fontina cheese**
- 1 **can (½ oz.) white truffles (optional)**

In the top of a double boiler, beat egg yolks and milk until well blended. Place over gently simmering water (water should just touch bottom of top unit). Cook, stirring constantly, just until mixture is thick enough to coat a metal spoon with a thick, velvety layer (7 to 8 minutes). If overcooked, custard mixture first begins to look grainy, then separates.

Immediately stir in cheese. Continue to cook, stirring, until all but a few shreds of cheese are smoothly melted. Remove double boiler from heat but leave sauce over hot water for about 10 minutes, stirring occasionally. If made ahead, cover and refrigerate for up to 5 days. To reheat, place over simmering water and stir until warmed through.

If using truffles, drain their juice into sauce. Then cut truffles into paper-thin slices; reserve a few slices for garnish and stir remainder into sauce. Serve sauce with vegetables, meat, poultry, or eggs as directed below. Makes about 2⅓ cups sauce.

FONDUTA WITH VEGETABLES

Prepare **Fonduta;** ladle over **hot cooked vegetables** such as broccoli, green beans, spinach, cauliflower, artichoke hearts or bottoms, asparagus, Italian green beans, celery, onions, leeks, or zucchini. Or spoon sauce over sautéed mushrooms, eggplant, or green or red bell peppers. Allow 2 to 3 tablespoons Fonduta for each ½ cup vegetables.

FONDUTA WITH VEAL OR CHICKEN

Prepare **Fonduta;** pass at the table to spoon over roasted, sautéed, or broiled **veal** (chops, roasts, or steaks) or chicken. Allow ¼ to ⅓ cup Fonduta for each serving (about ½ lb. boneless meat).

FONDUTA WITH EGGS

Prepare **Fonduta** and spoon over **poached eggs;** allow 3 tablespoons Fonduta for each egg.

CHEDDAR CHEESE SAUCE

- 2 **tablespoons butter or margarine**
- 2 **tablespoons all-purpose flour**
- 1 **cup milk**
- ½ **cup shredded Cheddar cheese**
  Salt and pepper

Melt butter in a 1½- to 2-quart pan over medium heat. Add flour and cook, stirring, until bubbly. Remove from heat and gradually stir in milk. Return to heat and cook, stirring constantly, until sauce boils and thickens. Add cheese and stir until melted. Season to taste with salt and pepper. Makes about 1 cup.

MORNAY SAUCE

Follow directions for **Cheddar Cheese Sauce,** but substitute ½ cup *each* **regular-strength beef broth** or chicken broth and **half-and-half** for milk. Substitute 2 tablespoons *each* grated **Parmesan cheese** and shredded **Gruyère or Swiss cheese** for Cheddar cheese. Substitute a dash of **ground red pepper** (cayenne) for black pepper.

Fonduta (facing page), northern Italy's eloquent answer to Swiss fondue, can be served
as a sauce for sautéed chicken or veal, or as a dip for cubes of crusty bread.
Here, the velvety fontina-based sauce tops chicken garnished with fluted mushrooms.

PASTA

The Italians made pasta and cheese an immortal combination long ago. The classics go on, but creative cooks continue to think of new variations on old themes.

◆ TAGLIARINI WITH CHÈVRE & OLIVES ◆

Warming any goat cheese enhances its flavor. Repeating this recipe with different goat cheeses reveals their variety.

- ¼ cup pine nuts
- 8 to 12 ounces soft, unripened chèvre (goat cheese)
- 2 cups *each* whipping cream and regular-strength chicken broth
- ½ cup Spanish-style or niçoise olives, pitted and chopped
- 8 ounces tagliarini
  Boiling salted water
- ¼ cup butter or margarine
- 3 teaspoons grated orange peel
- 3 tablespoons chopped chives
  Whole chives

Toast pine nuts in a small frying pan over medium heat until lightly browned (3 to 4 minutes), stirring constantly. Remove from heat and set aside.

Trim any coating from chèvre. Set chèvre aside. In a 4- to 5-quart pan, combine cream and broth. Bring to a boil; boil, uncovered, stirring occasionally, until reduced to 1½ cups. Reduce heat to low. Using a wire whisk, beat in about 8 ounces of the chèvre or enough to develop a rich chèvre flavor. (French chèvres are saltier, so you may want to use less than 8 ounces.) Stir in olives. Keep warm.

Following package directions, cook tagliarini in boiling salted water until *al dente*. Drain thoroughly. Melt butter in pan used to cook pasta; stir in pine nuts and 2 teaspoons of the orange peel, then add drained pasta. Mix gently by lifting with 2 forks.

Pour sauce into a serving bowl; mound pasta in center. Crumble remaining chèvre (about 4 ounces) and sprinkle over pasta; then sprinkle with chopped chives and remaining 1 teaspoon orange peel. Garnish with whole chives. Makes 6 to 8 first-course servings.

◆ RICOTTA GNOCCHI ◆

These light, spinach-flecked Italian dumplings get their smooth texture from mild ricotta cheese (see page 20). Top them with a simple sauce of fresh tomatoes cooked in broth.

Fresh Tomato Sauce (recipe follows)
- 2 packages (10 oz. *each*) frozen chopped spinach, thawed
- 1 pound ricotta cheese
- 2 eggs
- 1 cup fine dry bread crumbs
- 1 cup (about 5 oz.) grated Parmesan cheese
- 1 clove garlic, minced or pressed
- ½ teaspoon salt
  Dash of pepper
- ¼ teaspoon ground nutmeg
- 1 teaspoon dry basil
  All-purpose flour
  Boiling salted water
  Grated Parmesan cheese

Prepare Fresh Tomato Sauce and set aside.

Drain spinach well, then place in a colander and press out excess water. Place ricotta cheese in a large bowl. Beat in eggs, one at a time; then stir in bread crumbs, the 1 cup Parmesan cheese, garlic, salt, pepper, nutmeg, basil, and drained spinach. Mix very well. Shape mixture into 1½-inch balls. Roll balls in flour to coat lightly; arrange, slightly apart, on a baking sheet. (At this point, you may cover and refrigerate until next day.)

Gently drop half the gnocchi into a large pan of boiling salted water. When water returns to a boil, adjust heat so water boils very gently. Cook gnocchi for 10 minutes; remove from pan with a slotted spoon, drain well, place in a warm serving dish, and keep warm. Repeat with remaining gnocchi. To serve, reheat sauce and pour over gnocchi. Sprinkle with Parmesan cheese. Makes 8 main-dish servings.

Fresh Tomato Sauce. Melt 2 tablespoons **butter** or margarine in a 3-quart pan over medium heat. Add 1 large **onion,** chopped; cook, stirring, until soft. Stir in 3 large **tomatoes,** peeled, seeded, and chopped; 1 can (14½ oz.) **regular-strength chicken broth;** ½ teaspoon *each* **salt** and **dry basil;** and ⅛ teaspoon **pepper.** Increase heat to high. Bring to a boil; boil for 10 minutes, stirring occasionally. Then reduce heat to medium and simmer, uncovered, until sauce is reduced to about 2½ cups. Whirl sauce in a blender until smooth. If made ahead cover and refrigerate until next day.

TRUFFLE CANNELLONI WITH THREE CHEESES

Suitable for a first course or an entrée, this luxurious dish is worthy of the most special occasion. It's very rich, so keep the rest of the menu light.

- 2 tablespoons butter or margarine
- 1 large onion, finely chopped
- 2 large packages (8 oz. *each*) cream cheese, softened
- 1 cup (about 5 oz.) grated Parmesan cheese
- 3 cups (12 oz.) shredded fontina cheese
- ¼ cup whipping cream
- 1 small (at least ½ oz.) fresh or canned black or white truffle
- 6 egg roll skins

Melt butter in a wide frying pan over high heat. Add onion and cook, stirring, until golden (about 5 minutes). Remove from heat and set aside.

In large bowl of an electric mixer, beat cream cheese until smooth. Then beat in Parmesan cheese, 1 cup of the fontina cheese, cream, and onion mixture until well blended. Thinly sliver truffle and set aside. (If using a canned truffle, blend truffle liquid into cheese mixture.)

Spoon about ⅔ cup of the cheese mixture in a band at one side of each egg roll skin. Reserve about ¼ of the truffle slivers for garnish; sprinkle a few of remaining slivers over cheese on each egg roll. Roll up each skin to enclose filling. Place rolls, seam side down, side by side in a 9- by 13-inch baking dish. If serving as a first course, cut rolls in half crosswise. Sprinkle remaining 2 cups fontina cheese over rolls, covering egg roll skins completely. (At this point, you may cover rolls and reserved truffle slivers separately and refrigerate until next day. Bring to room temperature before baking.)

Bake, uncovered, in a 475° oven until cheese begins to brown around edges (about 10 minutes). Scatter reserved truffle slivers over top. Makes 12 first-course servings or 6 main-dish servings.

SAVORY BAKED NOODLES

The Italians have not quite cornered the market on cheese and pasta. This recipe goes back to the flavorful eastern European noodle kugel.

- 8 ounces spinach fettuccine
  Boiling salted water
- 1½ cups large curd cottage cheese
- 1 cup sour cream
- 1 clove garlic, minced or pressed
- 3 green onions (including tops), sliced
- 1 teaspoon Worcestershire
- ¼ teaspoon liquid hot pepper seasoning
- 2 tablespoons butter or margarine, melted
- ½ cup grated Parmesan cheese

Following package directions, cook fettuccine in boiling salted water until *al dente*. Drain well.

In a bowl, mix cottage cheese, sour cream, garlic, onions, Worcestershire, hot pepper seasoning, and butter. Gently stir in drained pasta. Turn into a greased 1½-quart casserole; sprinkle with Parmesan cheese. Bake in a 350° oven until heated through (about 30 minutes). Makes 4 to 6 side-dish servings.

GORGONZOLA FETTUCCINE

The truly bold will flavor this fettuccine with aged Gorgonzola. For a tamer dish, use one of the milder blues (see pages 10 and 11).

- ½ cup pine nuts
- 6 ounces Gorgonzola cheese
- 1½ cups whipping cream; or ¾ cup *each* milk and whipping cream
- ¼ cup butter or margarine
- 1 pound spinach fettuccine
  Boiling salted water
- ⅓ cup grated Parmesan cheese

Toast pine nuts in a small frying pan over medium heat until lightly browned (3 to 4 minutes), stirring constantly. Remove from heat and set aside.

Crumble Gorgonzola cheese with your fingers. Reserve ⅓ cup; place remaining Gorgonzola in an 8- to 10-inch frying pan and add cream and butter. Heat over low heat, stirring with a wire whisk, until mixture is smooth. Keep warm.

Following package directions, cook fettuccine in boiling salted water until *al dente*. Drain thoroughly, then transfer to a warm rimmed platter.

Pour sauce over pasta and sprinkle with Parmesan cheese. Mix gently by lifting pasta with 2 forks. Sprinkle with pine nuts and reserved Gorgonzola cheese. Makes 6 to 8 first-course servings or 4 main-dish servings.

The Italian genius for creating complicated flavors in simple dishes is
nowhere clearer than in Fettuccine with Four Cheeses (facing page). Fontina, Gorgonzola,
Bel Paese, and Parmesan enrich the simple cream sauce that dresses the pasta.

FETTUCCINE EMMENTHALER

This fettuccine is not only more delicate in flavor than Gorgonzola Fettuccine (page 77), but slightly less caloric as well.

- 10 ounces fettuccine or thin noodles
  Boiling salted water
- ½ cup (¼ lb.) butter or margarine, melted
- 2 cups (8 oz.) shredded imported Swiss cheese (Emmenthaler) or domestic Swiss cheese
  Freshly ground pepper
  Chopped parsley

Following package directions, cook fettuccine in boiling salted water until *al dente*. Drain pasta thoroughly and pour into a wide-rimmed pasta bowl or platter. Immediately add butter and 1 cup of the cheese; rapidly lift and toss pasta with 2 forks to blend in melting cheese. Sprinkle on remaining 1 cup cheese a little at a time, lifting pasta to mix in well. Sprinkle with pepper and parsley; serve at once. Makes about 4 main-dish servings.

FETTUCCINE WITH FOUR CHEESES

Photo on facing page

The four cheeses in this classic dish represent four families: firm, semisoft, blue, and grating.

- 3 tablespoons butter or margarine
- 1½ tablespoons all-purpose flour
- ⅛ teaspoon ground nutmeg
  Dash of white pepper
- 1 cup half-and-half or light cream
- ½ cup regular-strength chicken broth
- ⅓ cup *each* shredded fontina cheese and Bel Paese cheese
- ⅓ cup crumbled Gorgonzola cheese
- 8 ounces fettuccine
  Boiling salted water
  About 1 cup (about 5 oz.) grated Parmesan cheese

Melt 1½ tablespoons of the butter in a 2-quart pan over medium heat. Stir in flour, nutmeg, and white pepper; cook, stirring, until bubbly. Remove from heat and gradually stir in half-and-half and broth.

Return to heat and cook, stirring constantly, until sauce boils and thickens. Mix in fontina cheese and Bel Paese cheese; cook, stirring, until cheese is melted and sauce is smooth. Add Gorgonzola cheese and stir until blended. Keep warm. Or, if made ahead, let cool; then cover and refrigerate until next day. To reheat, place over simmering water and stir until smooth and heated through.

Following package directions, cook fettuccine in boiling salted water until *al dente*. Drain thoroughly, then toss lightly with remaining 1½ tablespoons butter and ½ cup of the Parmesan cheese. Spoon pasta onto serving plates; top equally with cheese sauce. Pass remaining Parmesan cheese at the table to sprinkle over individual servings. Makes about 6 first-course servings or 4 main-dish servings.

HAM MANICOTTI WITH CHEESE SAUCE

A kind of spicy deviled ham goes inside these manicotti; a creamy cheese sauce goes on top.

- 1 egg
- 1 cup small curd cottage cheese
- 2 cups ground cooked ham
- 2 green onions (including tops), finely chopped
- ½ teaspoon *each* rubbed sage, marjoram leaves, and Worcestershire
- ¼ teaspoon garlic salt
- 3 drops liquid hot pepper seasoning
  Cheese Sauce (recipe on page 80)
- 8 manicotti shells
  Boiling salted water
- ½ cup shredded Swiss cheese

In a large bowl, beat together egg and cottage cheese. Stir in ham, onions, sage, marjoram, Worcestershire, garlic salt, and hot pepper seasoning. Beat to blend well. Set aside.

Prepare Cheese Sauce and keep warm.

Following package directions, cook manicotti in boiling salted water until *al dente*. Drain, rinse under cold running water, and drain again. Stuff evenly with ham filling.

Spread ¼ of the Cheese Sauce in a 9- by 13-inch baking dish. Arrange filled manicotti, side by side, in sauce. Cover evenly with remaining sauce and sprinkle with Swiss cheese. (At this point, you may cover and refrigerate until next day. Bring to room temperature before baking.)

(Continued on next page)

Bake, covered, in a 350° oven for 20 minutes. Uncover; continue to bake until bubbly and heated through (about 10 more minutes). Makes 4 to 6 main-dish servings.

Cheese Sauce. Melt 3 tablespoons **butter** or margarine in a 1- to 1½-quart pan over medium heat. Stir in 3 tablespoons **all-purpose flour;** cook, stirring, until bubbly. Remove from heat and gradually stir in 1 cup **milk** and ½ cup **regular-strength chicken broth.** Return to heat and cook, stirring, until sauce boils and thickens. Stir in 1 tablespoon **tomato paste,** a dash *each* of **ground nutmeg** and **ground red pepper** (cayenne), and 2 tablespoons *each* shredded **Swiss cheese** and grated **Parmesan cheese.** Continue to cook, stirring, until cheese is melted.

◆ CAMEMBERT-STUFFED PASTA SHELLS ◆

As with Gorgonzola Fettuccine (page 77), the idea here is to use cheese to flavor pasta pungently.

    2 tablespoons butter or margarine
    1 small onion, chopped
    2 cloves garlic, minced or pressed
    8 ounces Camembert cheese (any rind removed), diced
    1 egg
    ½ cup ricotta cheese or small curd cottage cheese
    1 cup chopped parsley
    ½ cup grated Parmesan cheese
   25 to 30 large dried seashell-shaped pasta shells
       Boiling salted water
    1 jar (15 oz.) meatless spaghetti sauce or 2 cups homemade spaghetti sauce

Melt butter in an 8- to 10-inch frying pan over medium heat. Add onion and garlic and cook, stirring, until onion is soft. Reduce heat to low, add Camembert cheese, and stir until soft; remove from heat. In a small bowl, beat together egg, ricotta cheese, parsley, and ¼ cup of the Parmesan cheese; stir into Camembert mixture.

Following package directions, cook pasta shells in boiling salted water until *al dente.* Drain, rinse under cold running water, and drain again. Stuff shells evenly with cheese filling.

Spread half the spaghetti sauce in a 7- by 11-inch baking dish or shallow 2½-quart casserole. Arrange shells, filling side up, in sauce. Spoon

remaining sauce in a band over top of each. Bake, covered, in a 350° oven until hot and bubbly (about 30 minutes). Sprinkle with remaining ¼ cup Parmesan cheese. Makes 8 first-course or 4 main-dish servings.

◆ GERMAN-STYLE MACARONI & CHEESE ◆

To most Americans, macaroni and cheese is elbow pasta and Cheddar. This German-style variation features Swiss cheese, sausage, and spicy mustard.

    8 ounces elbow macaroni, rotelle, small seashell-shaped pasta, or bow-shaped pasta
       Boiling salted water
    4 tablespoons butter or margarine
       About ¾ pound garlic sausages or kielbasa (Polish sausage), thinly sliced
    2 large onions, chopped
    ¼ cup all-purpose flour
    2 cups milk
    4 teaspoons prepared German-style or other spicy mustard
    ½ teaspoon caraway seeds
    ¼ teaspoon white pepper
       Salt
    3 cups (12 oz.) shredded Swiss cheese

Following package directions, cook macaroni in boiling salted water until *al dente;* drain thoroughly.

Melt 1 tablespoon of the butter in a wide frying pan over medium heat. Add sausage slices and cook, stirring, until browned. Remove sausage from pan and set aside.

Melt remaining 3 tablespoons butter in pan. Add onions and cook, stirring, until soft. Stir in flour and cook until bubbly. Remove from heat and gradually stir in milk. Return to heat; cook, stirring constantly, until sauce boils and thickens. Remove from heat and stir in mustard, caraway seeds, white pepper, and drained macaroni; stir until well mixed. Season to taste with salt.

Pour half the macaroni mixture into a buttered shallow 2½-quart baking dish. Evenly distribute half the sausage, then half the cheese over macaroni. Layer on remaining macaroni mixture, then sausage, and then cheese. (At this point, you may let cool, then cover and refrigerate until next day.)

Bake, uncovered, in a 400° oven until cheese is bubbly and center of casserole is hot (about 25 minutes; about 35 minutes if refrigerated). Makes 4 to 6 main-dish servings.

PAIRING WINES & CHEESES

Wine and cheese—the two noblest products of fermentation—have been companions at table since Western civilization began. For some people, pairing them to get the subtlest nuances of flavor from each is almost an art. However, easy enjoyment can come from literally thousands of combinations. This chart shows a few starting points.

WINES		Gorgonzola	Stilton	Roquefort & other blues	Brie	Camembert	Cheddar	Hollanders	Chèvre	Monastery	String	Swiss
LIGHT, FRUITY REDS	Burgundy or red table	●	●	●	●	●	●	●	●	●	●	●
	Gamay			●	●	●	●	●	●	●	●	●
	Pinot Noir			●	●	●	●	●		●	●	●
	Light Zinfandels			●	●	●	●	●	●	●	●	●
DRY, FULL REDS	Cabernet Sauvignon				●	●	●	●				●
	Merlot				●	●	●	●			●	●
	Petite Sirah	●	●	●	●	●	●					●
	Full Zinfandels	●	●	●	●	●	●					●
PINK	Blanc de Noir				●		●	●		●		●
	Rosé				●		●			●		●
LIGHT, FRUITY WHITES	Chablis or white table				●		●	●	●	●	●	●
	Chenin Blanc						●					●
	French Colombard							●				●
	Gewürztraminer			●	●					●		●
	White Riesling									●		●
DRY, FULL WHITES	Chardonnay				●	●	●	●				
	Sauvignon Blanc				●		●	●	●			
	Semillon				●	●	●	●			●	●
SWEET WHITES	Light, sweet Muscat				●			●				
	Late harvest whites				●	●		●				
SHERRIES	Pale dry sherry					●	●	●				●
	Golden sherry					●	●	●				●
	Cream sherry						●	●				●
PORTS	Angelica	●	●			●	●	●				●
	Tawny port	●	●			●	●	●				●
	Ruby port	●	●				●					●

◆ LASAGNE PINWHEELS ◆

Pictured on facing page

The ingredients are all familiar, but this delightful version of the classic is far from traditional in shape.

    Tomato Sauce (recipe follows)
1   large bunch (about 1½ lbs.) spinach; or 1 package (10 oz.) frozen chopped spinach, thawed
1   pound ricotta cheese
1   cup (4 oz.) shredded mozzarella or jack cheese
½   cup grated Parmesan cheese
1   egg
¼   teaspoon *each* pepper and ground nutmeg
    Salt
8   lasagne noodles
    Boiling salted water

Prepare Tomato Sauce and set aside.

Discard tough stems from spinach. Rinse leaves well; place leaves, with water that clings to them, in a 4-quart pan. Cook over medium heat, stirring often, just until leaves are wilted (about 3 minutes). Drain and let cool, then place in a colander and press out excess water. Finely chop spinach. (If using thawed frozen spinach, drain spinach well, then press out excess water.)

In a large bowl, stir together spinach, ricotta cheese, mozzarella cheese, Parmesan cheese, egg, pepper, and nutmeg. Season to taste with salt. Set aside.

Following package directions, cook lasagne noodles in boiling salted water until *al dente*. Drain, rinse under cold running water, and place in a large bowl of ice water.

Pour Tomato Sauce into a greased shallow 3-quart casserole. To assemble pinwheels, pat each noodle dry with a clean dishtowel, then cut in half lengthwise. Spread about ¼ cup of the cheese mixture over each noodle half; roll up each noodle half jelly roll style, starting with a short end. Stand pinwheels, curly edges up, in casserole. Cover and bake in a 350° oven until heated through (about 30 minutes). Makes about 6 main-dish servings.

Tomato Sauce. Heat 3 tablespoons **olive oil** or salad oil in a wide frying pan over medium heat. Add 1 medium-size **onion,** chopped, and 1 large clove **garlic,** minced or pressed. Cook, stirring, until onion is soft. Add 1 large can (about 28 oz.) **pear-shaped tomatoes** (break up with a spoon) and their liquid. Reduce heat and simmer, uncovered, stir-ring occasionally, until sauce is reduced and thickened (15 to 20 minutes). If desired, stir in 2 tablespoons *each* minced **parsley** and minced **fresh basil.**

◆ LASAGNE BELMONTE ◆

This southern Italian version of lasagne cooks ahead beautifully, making it a great choice for entertaining. For a spicier flavor, substitute sausage for part of the beef.

3   tablespoons olive oil or salad oil
1   medium-size onion, chopped
1   clove garlic, minced or pressed
1½ pounds lean ground beef; or 1 pound lean ground beef and ½ pound mild Italian sausages
2   cans (8 oz. *each*) tomato sauce
1   can (6 oz.) tomato paste
½   cup *each* dry red wine and water
1   teaspoon *each* salt and oregano leaves
½   teaspoon *each* pepper and sugar
8   ounces lasagne noodles
    Boiling salted water
1   pound ricotta cheese or 2 cups small curd cottage cheese
8   ounces mozzarella cheese, thinly sliced
½   cup grated Parmesan cheese

Heat oil in a wide frying pan over medium heat. Add onion and garlic; cook, stirring, until onion is soft. Crumble in beef. (If using sausage, remove casings and crumble meat into pan along with beef.) Cook, stirring, until meat is browned. Spoon off and discard excess fat. Stir in tomato sauce, tomato paste, wine, water, salt, oregano, pepper, and sugar. Reduce heat, cover, and simmer for 45 minutes to 1 hour.

Following package directions, cook noodles in boiling salted water until *al dente*. Drain, rinse under cold running water, and drain again. Set aside.

Spread a thin layer of sauce over bottom of a buttered 9- by 13-inch baking dish. Arrange ⅓ of the drained noodles in an even layer over sauce. Spread ⅓ of remaining sauce over noodles; dot with ⅓ of the ricotta cheese, then cover with ⅓ of the mozzarella cheese. Repeat layers 2 more times. Sprinkle Parmesan cheese over top. (At this point, you may cover and refrigerate until next day.)

Bake, uncovered, in a 350° oven until bubbly and heated through (about 40 minutes; about 50 minutes if refrigerated). Cut into squares to serve. Makes 8 servings.

In Lasagne Pinwheels (facing page), a familiar dish takes a surprising new form.
Instead of lying flat in the baking dish, the frilly-edged noodles
are spread with a cheese mixture, then rolled up into elegant blossoms.

BREADS

In much the same way that cheese can bring subtle flavors to soufflés, it can be used to make bread take on unexpected new flavors and textures.

SURPRISE BREAD BUNDLES

The surprise is a creamy cheese filling, either sweet or savory.

    1 package active dry yeast
    ¼ cup warm water (110° F)
    ½ cup (¼ lb.) butter or margarine, melted
       and cooled
    ¼ cup half-and-half, light cream, or milk
    1 teaspoon ground nutmeg
    ½ teaspoon salt
    3 tablespoons sugar (omit if using Savory
       Cheese Filling)
    4 eggs
    4 to 4¼ cups all-purpose flour
       Sweet Cheese Filling or Savory Cheese
       Filling (recipes follow)
    1 tablespoon water

In large bowl of an electric mixer, dissolve yeast in warm water. Let stand for 5 minutes. In a small bowl, stir together butter, half-and-half, nutmeg, salt, and sugar (if used); add to yeast mixture along with 3 of the eggs and 2 cups of the flour. Stir to blend, then beat on medium speed for 2 minutes.

If using a heavy-duty mixer with a dough hook, gradually mix in 1¾ to 2 cups more flour; beat on medium speed until dough pulls away from bowl sides. If not using a heavy-duty mixer, beat in flour with a heavy spoon. Scrape dough out onto a board sprinkled with about ¼ cup flour. Knead until smooth and satiny (5 to 10 minutes), adding more flour as needed to prevent sticking. Place dough in a greased bowl; turn over to grease top. Cover; let rise in a warm place until doubled (about 2 hours).

Punch down dough, turn out onto a floured board, and knead briefly to release air. Wrap airtight and refrigerate until dough is thoroughly chilled (at least 2 hours or until next day). Meanwhile, prepare filling of your choice.

Knead chilled dough briefly to release air, then divide into 16 equal portions. Shape each portion into a 6- to 6½-inch circle. Place 1/16 of the filling (2 to 2½ tablespoons) in center of each circle. Draw dough up around filling and pleat edges to take up excess; then pinch pleats together firmly just above filling, letting dough top flare loosely. Place shaped bundles 2 inches apart on greased 10- by 15-inch baking sheets; cover loosely and keep cold until all dough has been shaped.

Let covered bundles rise in a warm place until puffy (about 30 minutes). Uncover. To seal firmly, lightly pinch pleats together again. Lightly beat together remaining egg and the 1 tablespoon water; brush over bundles. Bake in a 350° oven until golden brown (about 25 minutes). Serve warm or at room temperature. If made ahead, cool completely on racks; then wrap airtight and freeze for up to 6 months. To reheat, thaw bundles unwrapped; set slightly apart on a baking sheet and place in a 325° oven for about 20 minutes. Serve with butter. Makes 16 bundles.

Sweet Cheese Filling. In a medium-size bowl, beat together 2 large packages (8 oz. *each*) **cream cheese,** softened; ½ cup **powdered sugar;** 1 **egg;** 2 teaspoons grated **fresh orange peel;** and ¼ teaspoon **almond extract.** Stir in 1 cup **raisins** and ½ cup chopped **candied orange peel.** If made ahead, cover and refrigerate until next day. Bring to room temperature before using.

Savory Cheese Filling. In a medium-size bowl, beat together 1 large package (8 oz.) **cream cheese,** softened; 8 ounces **feta cheese,** crumbled; 1 **egg;** and 1 cup finely chopped **green onions** (including tops). If made ahead, cover and refrigerate until next day. Bring to room temperature before using.

CHEESE & BACON CORN MUFFINS

Rich with Cheddar, these muffins make tasty company for chili.

    ½ pound bacon, diced
    1 cup chopped onion
    1¼ cups all-purpose flour
    ¾ cup yellow cornmeal
    ⅓ cup sugar
    3½ teaspoons baking powder
    1 teaspoon salt
    2 eggs
    1 cup milk
    3 tablespoons butter or margarine, melted
    1¼ cups (5 oz.) shredded sharp Cheddar
       cheese

In a wide frying pan, cook bacon over medium heat until crisp, stirring constantly. Lift out bacon with a slotted spoon. Pour off and discard all but 2 tablespoons drippings. Add onion to drippings in pan; cook, stirring, until soft.

In a large bowl, stir together flour, cornmeal, sugar, baking powder, and salt. In another bowl, beat together eggs, milk, and butter; add to flour mixture and stir just until dry ingredients are evenly moistened. Mix in bacon, onion, and ¾ cup of the cheese. Spoon batter into greased large (2¾- to 3-inch) muffin cups, filling cups ⅔ full. Sprinkle muffins evenly with remaining ½ cup cheese.

Bake in a 400° oven until a wooden pick inserted in center of muffins comes out clean (about 20 minutes). Turn muffins out of pans onto racks. Serve warm. Makes 16 to 18 muffins.

◆ GOUGÈRE ◆

This great Burgundian cheese pastry elevates the cream puff to new heights. With red wine and green salad, it makes an excellent lunch.

    1   cup milk
    ¼   cup butter or margarine
    ¼   teaspoon salt
        Dash of white pepper
    1   cup all-purpose flour
    4   eggs
    1   cup (4 oz.) shredded Gruyère or Swiss
        cheese

Heat milk and butter in a 3-quart pan over medium-high heat, stirring until butter is melted. Add salt and white pepper and bring to a rolling boil. Add flour all at once and beat with a wooden spoon until mixture leaves sides of pan and forms a ball (about 2 minutes). Remove from heat. Add eggs, one at a time, beating mixture until smooth after each addition. (Mixture will break apart into slippery clumps after each egg is added, but it will become a smooth paste again after vigorous beating.) Beat in ½ cup of the cheese.

Scoop out 7 mounds of dough with an ice cream scoop or a large spoon, using about ¾ of the dough. Arrange mounds, sides barely touching, in a circle on a greased baking sheet. Scoop remaining dough into 7 smaller mounds, placing one atop each larger mound. Sprinkle remaining ½ cup cheese over all.

Bake on center rack of a 375° oven until puffs are browned and crisp (about 50 minutes). Serve immediately. Makes 7 servings.

◆ DOUBLE CHEESE BREAD ◆

The interplay of different flavors makes the cheese board a fascinating taste experience, and so it is with this Cheddar and blue cheese quick bread.

    3   cups all-purpose flour
    1   cup whole wheat flour
    4   teaspoons baking powder
    ½   teaspoon baking soda
    1   teaspoon salt
  1½   cups chopped walnuts
    ⅔   cup butter or margarine, softened
  1⅓   cups sugar
    4   eggs
    ⅔   cup *each* milk and dry white wine; or 1⅓
        cups milk
  1½   cups (6 oz.) shredded sharp Cheddar
        cheese
    1   cup (4 oz.) crumbled blue-veined cheese
    1   tablespoon poppy seeds
    1   tablespoon sesame seeds

Stir together all-purpose flour, whole wheat flour, baking powder, baking soda, salt, and walnuts. Set aside.

In large bowl of an electric mixer, cream butter and sugar until fluffy. Add eggs, one at a time, beating well after each addition. Stir flour mixture into creamed mixture alternately with milk and wine. Spoon half the batter into another bowl. Stir Cheddar cheese into one portion of batter, blue cheese into other portion.

Spoon half the Cheddar cheese batter into each of 2 greased, flour-dusted 5- by 9-inch loaf pans, distributing batter down one long side of each pan. Then spoon half the blue cheese batter into each pan alongside Cheddar batter. Sprinkle poppy seeds over Cheddar batter; sprinkle sesame seeds over blue cheese batter.

Bake in a 350° oven until a wooden pick inserted in center of loaf comes out clean (about 1 hour). Let cool in pans for 10 minutes, then turn loaves out onto racks to cool completely. If made ahead, wrap cooled loaves airtight in plastic wrap and freeze for up to 2 months. Let thaw unwrapped.

To serve, cut bread into ¾-inch-thick slices; it has a tendency to crumble. If you like, cut slices in half lengthwise. Makes 2 loaves.

Note: If you prefer, you can make one Cheddar loaf and one blue cheese loaf; just put all the Cheddar batter in one pan, all the blue cheese batter in another pan. Bake as directed.

Deliciously rich Old-fashioned Cheesecake (facing page) is reminiscent of
the one Grandma used to make with her own fresh cream cheese.
Your choice of raspberry or blueberry sauce dresses up each slice.

SWEET TREATS

The faint tang and unctuous smoothness of fresh cheeses—cream, farmers, ricotta, and their kin—combine perfectly with the juicy sweetness of fresh fruits to make some of the world's best and simplest desserts. Classics such as traditional cheesecake, blintzes, and cheese strudel also rely on these fresh cheeses for richness without cloying sweetness.

◆ CHEESE STRUDEL ◆

Middle Eastern fila dough mates neatly with soft, mild farmers cheese to make an old European standby, the strudel.

Strudel Filling (recipe follows)
8 sheets fila pastry, thawed if frozen
6 tablespoons butter or margarine, melted
¼ cup sugar

Prepare Strudel Filling and set aside. Lay fila sheets out flat on a large surface; cover with plastic wrap to prevent drying.

Brush one sheet of fila with some of the butter; stack 3 more sheets on top, brushing each with butter. Sprinkle 2 tablespoons of the sugar in a strip down one long side of top sheet of fila; strip should be about 1½ inches in from side of pastry and should extend to within 1 inch of ends.

Spoon half the filling evenly atop sugar. Fold ends of fila over filling; then fold side over filling and roll up jelly roll style. Carefully place roll, seam side down, on a lightly greased baking sheet. Brush all over with butter.

Repeat with remaining fila, butter, sugar, and filling to make a second strudel. Bake in a 375° oven until lightly browned (about 20 minutes). To serve, cut into slices with a serrated knife. Makes 2 rolls (8 to 10 servings *total*).

Strudel Filling. In a bowl, stir together 2 tablespoons **currants** and 1 tablespoon **brandy;** set aside. In large bowl of an electric mixer, combine ½ pound (about 1 cup) **farmers cheese** or dry curd cottage cheese, 3 **egg yolks,** 1 small package (3 oz.) **cream cheese** (softened), and ½ cup **sugar.** Beat until smooth. Stir in currant-brandy mixture and 1 teaspoon grated **lemon peel.**

◆ OLD-FASHIONED CHEESECAKE ◆

Pictured on facing page

The key to a pleasing texture lies in bringing the cream cheese to room temperature ahead of time, so it is very soft for mixing.

Sweet Butter Pastry (recipe on page 88)
2½ pounds fresh cream cheese or 5 large packages (8 oz. *each*) cream cheese, softened
1½ cups sugar
6 eggs
¼ cup all-purpose flour
2 teaspoons grated lemon peel
½ teaspoon *each* salt and ground nutmeg
4 teaspoons vanilla
½ cup whipping cream
Raspberry Sauce or Blueberry Sauce (recipes on page 88)
1½ cups sour cream
3 tablespoons sugar

Prepare pastry. Press ⅓ of the pastry over bottom of a 10-inch spring-form pan with sides removed. Bake in a 400° oven until pale golden (5 to 6 minutes); place on a rack and let cool. Butter pan sides and attach to pan bottom. Press remaining pastry up pan sides to within ¼ inch of rim. Set aside. Reduce oven heat to 325°.

In large bowl of an electric mixer, beat cream cheese and the 1½ cups sugar until soft and smooth; then beat in eggs, one at a time. Add flour, lemon peel, salt, nutmeg, and 3 teaspoons of the vanilla; beat just until smooth (do not overbeat). Stir in whipping cream. Pour filling into prepared crust and bake in a 325° oven until a knife inserted halfway to center comes out clean (1¼ to 1½ hours). Check after 1 hour; if top is turning too brown, cover loosely with foil.

While cake is baking, prepare sauce of your choice; let cool, then cover and refrigerate. Stir together sour cream, the 3 tablespoons sugar, and remaining 1 teaspoon vanilla; set aside.

As soon as cake is done, gently spread sour cream mixture over top; return cake to oven. Turn off oven and leave door ajar several inches. Let cheesecake remain in cooling oven for 1 hour, then place on a rack. Let cool for 15 minutes; loosen crust from pan sides with a knife. Let cake cool to room temperature. Cover and refrigerate up to 2 days.

To serve, remove pan sides and place cake on a platter. Cut into thin wedges; pass sauce to top each slice. Makes 16 to 20 servings.

(Continued on next page)

Sweet Butter Pastry. In a food processor, whirl 1½ cups **all-purpose flour**, 3 tablespoons **sugar**, and ½ teaspoon grated **lemon peel** just until combined. Add ⅔ cup cold **butter** or margarine, cut into chunks; whirl until crumbs the size of small peas form. Add 1 **egg** and ¼ teaspoon **vanilla**; whirl until mixture begins to clump together (don't let it form a ball). Gather dough into a ball with your hands.

Raspberry Sauce. Thaw 3 packages (12 oz. *each*) **frozen lightly sweetened raspberries.** Press through a wire strainer set over a 2-quart pan. To strained raspberries in pan, add 3 tablespoons **light corn syrup**, 1½ tablespoons *each* **cornstarch** and **water** (stirred together), and ¾ cup **sugar.** Bring to a boil over medium heat, stirring; boil for 2 minutes. Remove from heat and let cool.

Blueberry Sauce. In a 2-quart pan, combine ⅓ cup **sugar** and 1 tablespoon **cornstarch.** Add ⅓ cup **water** and stir until smooth. Add 2 cups **fresh blueberries** (or frozen unsweetened berries, thawed) and 2 tablespoons **lemon juice.** Cook over medium heat, stirring, until mixture boils and thickens. Remove from heat and let cool.

◆ PEAR CRISP WITH CHEESE ◆

Sharp Cheddar sets off the mild flavor of juicy winter pears.

> 4 or 5 d'Anjou or Bosc pears
> 2 tablespoons lemon juice
> ½ cup *each* all-purpose flour and sugar
> ¼ teaspoon *each* salt and ground cinnamon
> ⅛ teaspoon ground nutmeg
> ¼ cup firm butter or margarine
> ⅔ cup shredded sharp Cheddar cheese
> Sweetened whipped cream or vanilla ice cream (optional)

Peel, core, and slice pears; you should have about 6 cups. Arrange pear slices in a greased 8- or 9-inch square baking dish; drizzle with lemon juice. In a bowl, stir together flour, sugar, salt, cinnamon, and nutmeg. Using a pastry blender or 2 knives, cut in butter until mixture is crumbly. Mix in cheese; sprinkle topping evenly over pears.

Bake, uncovered, in a 350° oven until pears are tender and topping is lightly browned (about 45 minutes). Serve warm or cool, with whipped cream or ice cream, if desired. Makes 4 to 6 servings.

◆ SUMMER CHEESE TORTE ◆

The delicate freshness of mascarpone marks the Italian original of this cool torte, but fresh cheese made from whipping cream and buttermilk can be just as pleasing. We suggest topping the torte with strawberries, but you might also try sliced fresh peaches or another summer fruit.

> 1 cup Fresh Cheese (recipe follows) or ½ pound (about 1 cup) mascarpone
> 3 eggs, separated
> 6 tablespoons sugar
> 4 to 6 tablespoons Marsala or rum
> 1 frozen pound cake (11 to 12 oz.), thawed, or 1 packaged pound cake (11 to 12 oz.)
> 1 to 2 cups strawberries

About 4 or 5 days ahead of time, prepare Fresh Cheese.

In large bowl of an electric mixer, beat egg whites on high speed until foamy. Gradually add 3 tablespoons of the sugar; continue to beat until mixture holds stiff peaks. In another bowl, combine egg yolks and remaining 3 tablespoons sugar. Beat until very thick. Place cheese in a large bowl; gradually add egg yolk mixture, beating until smoothly blended. Then fold egg white mixture into cheese mixture along with 2 tablespoons of the Marsala.

Cut cake crosswise into ¼-inch-thick slices. Line a pretty, wide dessert bowl (at least 12-cup size) with half the cake slices and sprinkle with 1 to 2 tablespoons more Marsala. Spoon cheese mixture into bowl, spreading evenly. Attractively arrange remaining cake slices on top; sprinkle with remaining 1 to 2 tablespoons Marsala.

Cover and refrigerate for at least 6 hours or until next day. Garnish with strawberries. Makes 8 to 10 servings.

Fresh Cheese. In a small pan over low heat, warm 1½ cups **whipping cream** to between 90° and 100°F. Stir in 2 tablespoons **buttermilk.** Pour into a glass or plastic container, cover, and let stand at room temperature (68° to 72°F) until a soft curd is formed (24 to 48 hours; mixture should look like soft yogurt). Curd forms faster in hot weather than in cool weather.

Cut a square of muslin, moisten with water, and wring dry. Use cloth to line a colander, draping excess over rim. Set lined colander in sink. Pour curd into colander and let drain for about 10 minutes. Fold cloth over curd; set colander on a rack in a rimmed pan. Cover entire unit airtight with plastic wrap and refrigerate until cheese is firm (36 to 48 hours). Makes 1 cup.

ALMOND-CHEESE COFFEECAKE

This brunch cake is aromatic with almonds and sweet from its glaze. The tender bread wraps around a smooth, rich cream cheese filling.

    1   package active dry yeast
    ¼   cup warm water (110°F)
    2   tablespoons sugar
    ½   teaspoon salt
        About 2½ cups all-purpose flour
    6   tablespoons firm butter or margarine
    2   egg yolks
    ½   cup milk
        Cheese Filling (recipe follows)
    ¼   cup sliced almonds
        Vanilla Glaze (recipe follows)

In a small bowl, dissolve yeast in warm water. Let stand for 5 minutes.

In large bowl of an electric mixer, combine sugar, salt, and 2 cups of the flour. Using a pastry blender or 2 knives, cut in butter until mixture resembles coarse crumbs.

Stir in yeast mixture, egg yolks, and milk; beat on medium speed until well blended. Stir in about ⅓ cup more flour or enough to make a soft dough. Turn dough out onto a floured board; shape into a ball. Place in a greased bowl; turn over to grease top. Cover with plastic wrap. Refrigerate for at least 6 hours or until next day. Meanwhile, prepare Cheese Filling.

Punch down dough, turn out onto a floured board, and knead briefly to release air. Roll dough out to a 10- by 13-inch rectangle, adding flour to board as needed to prevent sticking. Carefully transfer rectangle to a greased 14- by 17-inch rimless baking sheet. Spread filling over dough to within 1 inch of edges; sprinkle with almonds.

Starting from one long side of rectangle, roll dough jelly roll style just to center of rectangle. Repeat with other long side; shaped dough should now look like 2 jelly rolls side by side.

Using a floured knife, make cuts through one roll at a time, spacing cuts 1½ inches apart and cutting to center of roll. Gently lift and turn cut portions on their sides to expose filling. Cover and let rise in a warm place until very puffy (about 45 minutes). Bake in a 350° oven until top is golden brown (about 25 minutes). Prepare glaze and spread over coffeecake. Serve warm.

If made ahead, do not glaze warm cake. Place on a rack and let cool completely, then wrap in foil and freeze for up to 2 months. To reheat, unwrap cake; place on a baking sheet, cover with foil, and bake in a 350° oven until hot (about 15 minutes). Spread with glaze. Makes 6 to 8 servings.

Cheese Filling. In small bowl of an electric mixer, combine 1 large package (8 oz.) **cream cheese,** softened; ¼ cup **sugar;** 3 tablespoons **all-purpose flour;** 1 **egg yolk;** and 1 teaspoon *each* grated **lemon peel** and **almond extract.** Beat until smooth.

Vanilla Glaze. Stir together ½ cup **powdered sugar,** ¼ teaspoon **vanilla,** and 2 tablespoons **milk.**

CHEESE BLINTZES

Fruit topping—whether jam, preserves, or simply sliced fresh fruit—is the perfect complement for sweet cheese blintzes. Cherries are the traditional choice, but any favorite fruit tastes just as good.

    16 to 18 Sweet Crêpes (recipe follows)
    1   pound ricotta cheese
    2   tablespoons honey
    1   tablespoon lemon juice
    ½   teaspoon *each* grated lemon peel and
        ground cinnamon
    ⅛   teaspoon salt
        About 4 tablespoons butter or margarine
        Sweetened fresh fruit, jam, or preserves
        About 1 cup sour cream or plain yogurt
        (optional)

Prepare Sweet Crêpes and set aside.

In a small bowl, beat together ricotta cheese, honey, lemon juice, lemon peel, cinnamon, and salt. Spoon about 2 tablespoons of the ricotta mixture in center of each crêpe. Fold opposite sides of crêpe over filling to overlap slightly at center; then fold top and bottom in toward center to form a packet. Arrange folded crêpes, seam side down, on a baking sheet. (At this point, you may cover and refrigerate for up to 4 hours.)

Melt 2 tablespoons of the butter in a wide frying pan over medium heat. Arrange as many blintzes in pan as will fit without crowding, placing them seam side down. Cook, turning as needed, until golden brown on both sides (about 4 minutes *total*). Transfer to a platter and keep warm. Repeat with remaining blintzes, adding more butter to pan as needed. Serve blintzes with fruit; if desired, pass sour cream at the table to spoon over individual portions. Makes about 6 servings.

Sweet Crêpes. Prepare **Basic Crêpes** (page 66), but add 1 tablespoon **sugar** to the batter.

In France as well as other European countries, the major meal of the day often ends with a plate of fruits and cheeses. Cheese alone may be served in winter, when fresh fruit is scarce.

SELECTING THE CHEESES

The selection of cheeses for a cheese board can be something of an art, but the basic principles are easy: either you can serve one perfectly ripened cheese—as in the famous French quest after a Brie at the very hour of its pinnacle—or you can demonstrate on a single board how much variety cheese offers in texture and flavor.

On this continent, the quest for the perfect Brie is problematic, but the idea of serving a single fine cheese is just as sensible here as in France. Give it crusty bread or crackers (or both) and fresh fruit for company, and it will make a satisfying conclusion to a meal. Decorate the cheese board with fresh leaves (grape, lemon, ti, or fig), and few other desserts can match it in appearance.

Selecting a variety of cheeses for a pleasing board takes a little more thought, but it is not a daunting exercise. The point is to choose a range of textures from soft to firm, and a spectrum of flavors from sweet and mild to sharper and stronger. The easiest way to start is at the center, with a mild, semisoft cheese such as Bel Paese, and then work out toward as many extremes as your guests might appreciate. (Be sure to provide separate knives for the cheeses if they differ distinctly in flavor.)

Following is a traditional combination:

**Bel Paese   Brie   Danish Blue
Cheshire   Gruyère**

Bel Paese is semisoft and mild. Brie is a soft-ripened cheese, a distinctly flavored "bloomy rind." Danish Blue is also soft in texture and definite in flavor. The firm Cheshire belongs to the family of Cheddars, and Gruyère is a firm Swiss.

Immediately, one can begin imagining substitutions for each—St. Paulin for the Bel Paese, St. André for the Brie, Oregon Blue for the Dan-

ish Blue, Cougar Gold for the Cheshire, and Asiago or dry jack for the Gruyère.

Smaller groups succeed just as well. Here are three examples:

Cheddar   Port du Salut   Oregon Blue

Brie   Gruyère   Gorgonzola

Camembert   Fontina d'Aosta

A cheese board that focuses within a family is a bit more difficult to assemble. These two combinations have been suggested by an English authority:

**Danish Blue   Roquefort   Bleu de Bresse
mild Stilton   very ripe Stilton**

**Pont l'Évêque   Münster   Maroilles
Port du Salut   Reblochon**

A cheese board of this sort is something like a formal wine tasting; in order to succeed, it requires a table of seriously interested cheese fanciers. Among more casual tasters, however, the blue cheeses would probably appeal to a wider audience than the powerfully aromatic collection of semisofts, but both might be too much of a good thing.

ADDING THE FRUIT

Cheese is basically a product of temperate climates, and so are the fresh fruits that traditionally go with it. Grapes, apples, and pears lead the list, but many others work just as well. Also to be considered are figs, strawberries, melon, and kiwi fruit. The main exceptions are citrus and tropical fruits. The strong acidity of oranges and other citrus fruits tends to overwhelm the milder milk acids of cheese, and many tropical fruits are overbearingly aromatic.

A few fruit-and-cheese combinations are classic; two among them are Brie and apples, and pears and young Pecorino.

Put out separate knives for whole fruits needing to be sliced. Letting guests slice their own fruit at the table avoids the problem of browning.

A successful cheese board presents a variety of textures and flavors. Clockwise from
the top are California chèvre with paprika, pepper Brie, Pont l'Évêque, Cheddar-and-Stilton,
Banon (French chèvre), and Samsoe. Grapes and pears are traditional complements.

◆ PASKHA ◆

This westernized version of the great Russian Easter dessert starts with a tangy, absolutely fresh cheese made from buttermilk. Complement the cheese with juicy fruit (such as strawberries or pineapple) and plain cookies.

>   Candied Orange Peel (recipe follows) or
>   ½ cup chopped purchased candied
>   orange peel
> 1   gallon (4 qts.) buttermilk
> 1   cup whole unblanched almonds
> 1   cup (½ lb.) butter or margarine, softened
> 2   cups sour cream
> 2   eggs
> 1   cup sugar
> 2   teaspoons vanilla
> 1½ cups raisins; or 1½ cups pitted dates,
>   finely snipped
> 1   cup chopped dried apricots

Prepare Candied Orange Peel; chop enough to make ½ cup. Set aside.

Pour buttermilk into a heavy 5- to 6-quart pan. Warm over medium-low heat, stirring gently several times so buttermilk will heat evenly, until buttermilk reaches 185°F (20 to 30 minutes). Buttermilk will separate into curds and whey. Cut 2 pieces of cheesecloth; moisten with water, wring dry, and lay out flat, one on top of the other. Use cloth to line a fine-mesh strainer. Place strainer in sink; pour buttermilk mixture through strainer. Let stand until curds stop dripping (10 to 15 minutes).

Meanwhile, spread almonds in a 10- by 15-inch rimmed baking pan. Bake in a 350° oven until nuts are golden beneath skins (about 8 minutes; break one in half to check). Reserve 8 to 10 whole almonds for garnish. Coarsely chop remaining almonds and set aside.

In a large bowl, stir together buttermilk curds, butter, sour cream, eggs, and sugar. Place half the mixture in a food processor or blender; whirl until very smooth. Repeat with remaining mixture. Pour all mixture into a heavy 5- to 6-quart pan; cook over low heat, stirring frequently, until mixture reaches 140°F (about 20 minutes). Remove from heat. Blend in chopped almonds, vanilla, raisins, apricots, and orange peel.

Cut two 18-inch squares of cheesecloth; moisten with water, wring dry, and lay out flat, one on top of the other. Use cloth to smoothly line a 6- to 8-cup round basket with a flat bottom or a clean flowerpot. Drape excess cheesecloth over rim of basket. Arrange reserved almonds in a circle on bottom of basket.

Spoon cheese mixture into basket; fold excess cheesecloth over cheese mixture. To press cheese and force drainage, set a plate (one that fits inside top of basket) on cheese mixture; top with about 4 pounds of weights, such as canned goods. Set basket on a rack in a rimmed pan; cover entire unit airtight with plastic wrap. Refrigerate for at least 6 hours or up to 24 hours.

Remove weights from cheese; lift off plate. Fold excess cheesecloth back to expose cheese. Invert a serving plate over cheese; holding basket and plate together, invert cheese onto plate. Remove basket and pull off cheesecloth. Serve; or cover with plastic wrap and refrigerate for up to 3 days. Cut into wedges to serve. Makes 4 pounds paskha (12 to 16 servings).

Candied Orange Peel. With a vegetable peeler, pare off colored surface of peel of 3 large **oranges.** Combine peel and 3 cups **water** in a 1- to 2-quart pan. Bring to a boil; reduce heat and simmer, uncovered, for 15 minutes. Drain, discarding cooking water. Return peel to pan with ½ cup *each* **water** and **sugar.** Bring to a boil over high heat; boil, uncovered, stirring frequently, until peel is shiny and almost all liquid has evaporated (about 10 minutes). Lay peel on a rack and let cool. If made ahead, cover and refrigerate for up to 1 week.

◆ RICOTTA BERRY PIE ◆

The wonderfully silky texture of true ricotta makes berries seem all the juicier.

>   Flaky Butter Pastry (recipe follows)
> 2½ cups blackberries or boysenberries
> ¾   cup sugar
> 1½ tablespoons quick-cooking tapioca
> ¾   teaspoon ground cinnamon
> 8   ounces ricotta cheese
> 1   egg, separated
> ¼   teaspoon salt
> ½   cup half-and-half or light cream
> ¾   teaspoon grated lemon peel
> 1   tablespoon lemon juice

Prepare pastry. On a lightly floured board, roll out pastry and fit into a 9-inch pie pan. Trim pastry extending beyond pan rim to leave a ½-inch overhang. Fold overhang under itself and press lightly to seal, then flute edge of crust.

In a bowl, stir together berries, ½ cup of the sugar, tapioca, and ½ teaspoon of the cinnamon; let stand for 5 minutes. In a food processor or blender, whirl ricotta cheese, egg yolk, salt, half-and-half, remaining ¼ cup sugar, lemon peel, and lemon juice until smooth. In large bowl of an electric mixer, beat egg white until it holds soft, moist peaks; gently fold in cheese mixture.

Turn berry mixture into pastry shell; evenly spread cheese mixture on top. Sprinkle with remaining ¼ teaspoon cinnamon. Bake in a 425° oven for 10 minutes; then reduce oven heat to 350° and continue to bake until topping appears set when pan is gently shaken (about 30 more minutes). Place on a rack and let cool to room temperature. If made ahead, cover and refrigerate for up to 24 hours. Makes 6 servings.

Flaky Butter Pastry. Prepare **Pastry Dough** (page 64), but reduce flour to 1 cup and use only 6 tablespoons butter or margarine.

◆ CHEESE PASTRIES ◆

These tender little diamonds are a delectable version of an old Hungarian dessert pastry.

> **Buttery Pastry (recipe follows)**
> 1½ **pounds (about 3 cups) farmers cheese or dry curd cottage cheese**
> 5 **egg yolks**
> 1½ **cups granulated sugar**
> ¼ **teaspoon salt**
> 1 **teaspoon vanilla**
> ½ **cup golden raisins**
> **Grated peel of 1 lemon**
> 6 **egg whites**
> **Powdered sugar**

Prepare Buttery Pastry and divide in half. Cover one portion and set aside. Press remaining portion evenly over bottom of a 9- by 13-inch baking pan.

In a large bowl, combine cheese, egg yolks, ¾ cup of the granulated sugar, salt, and vanilla. Beat until smooth. Stir in raisins and lemon peel; set aside. In another large bowl, using clean, dry beaters, beat egg whites until they hold soft, moist peaks. Gradually beat in remaining ¾ cup granulated sugar and continue to beat until mixture is stiff and glossy. Fold egg white mixture into cheese mixture and spread in pastry-lined pan.

On a lightly floured board, roll out remaining pastry to a 9- by 13-inch rectangle and carefully place over cheese filling. With a fork, pierce pastry all over at 1-inch intervals.

Bake in a 350° oven until pastry is lightly browned (about 1 hour). Sprinkle lightly with pow-

dered sugar and cut into 2- by 2½-inch diamonds. Makes about 2 dozen pastries.

Buttery Pastry. Place 2 cups **all-purpose flour** in a bowl. Using a pastry blender or 2 knives, cut in 1 cup (½ lb.) firm **butter** or margarine until mixture resembles coarse crumbs. Stir in 1 **egg yolk.** Gradually sprinkle in 2 to 4 tablespoons **milk,** stirring with a fork until dough holds together.

◆ COEUR À LA CRÈME ◆

Pictured on page 94

Use the traditional heart-shaped ceramic mold or a natural-finish basket to form this simple dessert.

> **Vanilla Sugar (recipe follows) or sugar**
> 1 **quart whole milk**
> ¼ **cup buttermilk**
> **Plain cookies**
> **Fresh fruit, such as strawberries, raspberries, or cherries**

Prepare Vanilla Sugar.

In a small pan over low heat, warm milk to between 90° and 100°F. Stir in buttermilk. Pour into a glass or plastic container; cover and let stand at room temperature (68° to 72°F) until mixture begins to thicken—12 to 16 hours. (Or use a yogurt maker; thickening time is about the same.)

To shape cheese, use one 2-cup heart-shaped mold or four ½-cup heart-shaped molds; or use plain molds of the same volume. For each mold, cut 2 squares of cheesecloth; moisten with water, wring dry, and lay out flat, one on top of the other. Smoothly line mold (or molds) with cloth, draping excess cloth over mold rims. Pour thickened milk mixture into mold or molds and loosely fold cloth over cheese. Set on a rack in a rimmed pan. Cover entire unit airtight with plastic wrap and refrigerate for at least 24 hours or up to 2 weeks to allow flavor to develop and cream to thicken further.

To serve, unfold cloth to expose cheese. Invert a serving plate over cheese; then, holding plate and mold together, invert cheese onto plate. (Turn small molds out onto individual plates.) Lift off mold and gently pull off cloth. Sprinkle cheese with Vanilla Sugar and accompany with cookies and fruit. Makes 4 servings.

Vanilla Sugar. Place 1 **vanilla bean** in a 1-quart jar. Fill jar with **sugar.** Cover tightly and let stand for at least 2 days so flavor of bean permeates sugar. Replenish sugar as it is used; bean will give off flavor for several years.

INDEX

The first luscious cherries and strawberries of the season are perfect companions for the classic French dessert called Coeur à la Crème (page 93). Spread the creamy cheese on petit beurre biscuits or other plain cookies.

METRIC CONVERSION TABLE

To Change	To	Multiply by
ounces (oz.)	grams (g)	28
pounds (lbs.)	kilograms (kg)	0.45
teaspoons	milliliters (ml)	5
tablespoons	milliliters (ml)	15
fluid ounces (fl. oz.)	milliliters (ml)	30
cups	liters (l)	0.24
pints (pt.)	liters (l)	0.47
quarts (qt.)	liters (l)	0.95
gallons (gal.)	liters (l)	3.8
Fahrenheit temperature (°F)	Celsius temperature (°C)	5/9 after subtracting 32